The Day the Dollar Died

The Day the Dollar Died

A Novel

Robert V. Baynes

*For my mother who was the first to read
the rough draft of this book and had given me
great suggestions.*

Chapter 1

The branches on the tree at the end of the field were swaying in the wind as if daring the budding leaves to emerge completely. Even though the sun shone brightly, the green John Deere tractor had its cab closed up tightly.

Inside the cab, John Bower had on a slightly worn, brown coverall coat. As the tractor made its way slowly down the field, the brown earth yielded to the sixteen-row planter.

John's salt and pepper hair showed through the cab as his calloused hands steered the tractor in a straight line toward the road. Nearly half of the eighty-acre field had lines from the planter etched onto it.

The sun hung low on the horizon as the tractor neared the road. An approaching cloud of dust on the stone road signaled a moving vehicle.

As the cloud of dust drew nearer, a five-year-old brown Chevy SUV appeared. It pulled to the side of the road next to the field. As the dust cleared away, a five-foot-three woman emerged from the driver's side door.

She looked slim, wore blue jeans, and a thigh-length coat with a belt that accented her narrow waist. Her auburn hair came almost to her shoulders.

She nimbly made her way to the edge of the field and waited for the green tractor to make its way toward her.

As the tractor came to a halt, John opened the door. "Hi, Honey!" he yelled.

"Hey good looking, want something to eat?"

"Boy, am I glad to see you!"

"C'mon before it gets cold."

As he opened the door, the aroma of homemade meatloaf met him. He took in a deep breath. "Anna that smells *really* good!"

"John, you always say that."

"I mean it. You're one of the best cooks."

"Flattery will get you --- *everywhere!*" she giggled.

John chuckled and stuffed a forkful of food into his mouth.

"How's it going?" Anna asked.

"Mphf, pret goo so fer"

"Will you be late tonight?"

"Not too late. Just wanna finish this field."

"I'll be waiting for you."

"Oh? I'll look forward to that!"

As John took his last bite, he wiped his mouth and opened the door. "Better get the tractor going. Be home as soon as I can."

Darkness reigned by the time he pulled the tractor onto the road. A quarter-mile down the road a mailbox shaped like a barn appeared. As he turned the tractor down the lane, the headlights illuminated the neatly trimmed front yard.

The first building to appear was a well-kept white farmhouse that had carefully been added on to several times. The original hip roof barn displayed red steel siding and had white trim all around.

Two white pole barns were just behind the house with a large grain bin just behind them. John pulled the tractor near the front of the first pole barn and quickly climbed down.

He walked past his garden. Even in the moonlight, the neat rows of seedlings could be seen. He walked into the garage as he pulled off his coat. He entered the mudroom and hung his coat up and took off his shoes.

As he stepped into the living room, he could hear Anna in the kitchen putting dishes away. He quietly walked across the hardwood floor to the kitchen doorway and saw her placing pans in the cupboard.

He walked up behind her and kissed her neck. "Is that you, Fransisco?" she said. "John could be home at any time."

"Real funny, Honey!"

"What do you expect when you sneak up on a helpless woman?"

"You smell good."

"Can't say the same for you."

"I'll get a shower."

"That would be nice."

As he stepped out of the bathroom, he noticed the house seemed quiet. He walked into their bedroom and saw Anna already with her eyes closed and breathing peacefully.

"She must have been more tired than I thought," He said to himself. He turned out the light and crawled into bed. He gave her a kiss on the cheek before turning over and going to sleep.

The next morning, he woke before daylight and turned on his light beside the bed. He looked around their tastefully decorated bedroom and noticed that Anna had already left the bed.

The sound of a spatula rubbing against a skillet accompanied the smell of eggs and toast.

John pulled on his jeans and white t-shirt and then made his way to the kitchen.

"Morning, Honey," he said as he looked in the kitchen doorway.

"Morning. Will you be heading out early?"

John pulled out a chair as he replied, "Yeah, I wanna make the best of this dry weather."

Anna placed a plate of scrambled eggs, fried potatoes, and toast in front of him and a smaller plateful across the table.

She sat down opposite him. He bowed his head and prayed, "Lord, thank You for our food, thank You for Anna and our family, and thank You for another day to serve You. Amen."

He ate quietly at first. "You been thinking again?" Anna queried.

"Yeah."

"Bout the government?"

"Yeah."

"What's botherin' you now?"

John shook his head, "All this stupid regulation and paperwork."

"Like what?"

"With the USDA, the EPA, the FDA, and all the others, it's like an alphabet soup of idiots!"

"Tell me how you really feel." she laughed.

"A few years ago, they said you had to be licensed just to spread manure!"

"I remember."

John scoffed, "They were even talking about trying to regulate dust!"

"That's silly!"

"I'm tryin' to farm organic, but the inspections and paperwork are ridiculous."

"I know," Anna shrugged, "not much you can do about it though."

"You're right. Just upset."
"Yeah, I know."

"Better get out in the field."

"Bye."

John put on his coat and left the house. As he walked toward the barn, he could see the fields stretching out past the two white pole barns.

He walked past his garden again and stopped to observe the small plants that were just beginning to grow.

"Why can't the rest of the world be neat and orderly with everything working together like this?" he asked under his breath.

As he made the rest of the way to his tractor, he looked over the neatly trimmed yard with perfect circles of mulch around every tree.

He also admired the flower beds that Anna had been planting.

The rain hit around 7:00 that evening and cut short John's planting. He drove the tractor home through the rain and parked in front of the barn again.

He pulled his coat over his head and ran for the house.

As soon as he entered the house, he could smell the fried chicken. "That smells good!" he said.
"It's ready soon as you wash up."

"Be right there!"

After washing and straightening his hair, he headed to the table. The fried chicken, mashed potatoes, and green beans were already on the table.

"Did you get a lot planted?" Anna asked.

"Got almost 200 acres planted so far. Soon half done,"

"That's good."

"Man, these beans are tasty! So's everything else."

Anna grinned, "Thanks, Hon."

"S'posed to warm up this weekend."

"That's good. Save room for dessert."

John raised his eyebrows, "What's for dessert?"

"Your favorite - blueberry crisp."

"Always got room for that."

"Been worrying about what the government will do to you next?"
John sighed, "I always worry about that. I think government intelligence is an oxymoron."

"I know. Will you probably be going to bed early tonight?"

"Maybe. I hoped to spend some quality time with you. Been a while."

"That might work, but you take a shower first."

"Yes, ma'am."

John showered and put on some cologne. When he stepped out of the bathroom, the house was silent. "Anna?" he questioned.

"I'm in here," she called from the bedroom.

He was heading toward the bedroom when the doorbell rang. "Who could that be?" he said barely loud enough for Anna to hear.

He pulled on the pants he carried and slipped his shirt over his head. Then he headed for the front door.

As he opened the door a man wearing a flannel shirt and blue jeans stood there. He stood about six feet tall and had dark brown hair with blue eyes.

John paused for a second and then said, "Jim Rush, what are you doing here this late at night?"
"John, I felt like I should talk to you about something. I know I don't know you real well, but could I step in for a minute?"

John opened the door wider, "Yeah, I guess."

"I s'pose at this time of night, I better get right to the point, huh?"

"Well, I am curious why you're here."

"I know you're a Christian man, so I think I can share with you how I feel."

"Yeah, sure."

"I think God is leading me to ask if you want to buy my tractor." Jim shifted his weight and stared at the floor, "I could make a real good deal for ya. Just take over my payments and in about a year, it'll be paid for."

"Why not just trade it in if you're getting a new one?"

"John, I'm selling out. I don't need a new one."

John furrowed his brow, "Selling out? What in the world for?"

"It's a long story."

"Can you give it to me in a nutshell?"

"Well, John, I think I'm leaving the country."

John's eyes widened, "Why would you do that?!"

"Our national debt is soaring, nobody in Washington is doing anything about it, and the economic situation in the rest of the country is deteriorating also."

"I know things are bad, but this is America! I can't imagine things could get so bad you have to leave."

"I'm quite certain we'll see martial law here and lose our property rights." Jim squared his shoulders, "I've looked at this for a while and I think this is what I have to do."

"Where would you go?"

"I've been looking at a few countries in South America."

"Wow, I can't believe it! Just selling out and leaving, huh?" John lifted his hands in confusion.

"I know it sounds extreme."

"Well, I've been thinking about getting a new tractor anyway."

"Maybe this is why I felt I should talk to you."

"Let me give you my email address. If you do leave, could you email me and let me know how things are going?" John jotted it down on the back of an envelope.

"Sure, maybe you could come visit sometime," he said as he headed toward his truck.

After John closed the front door, he went to the bedroom and Anna asked, "Who could that have been?"

"Jim Rush from over on 700 South."

"What did he want at this time of night?"

John explained to her what they had talked about, then added, "Sounds kind of radical to me."

"He might be the sanest one of all of us."

"Do you wanna leave too?"

Anna shook her head, "No, I couldn't leave the grandkids."

"I agree. Now, where were we before we were interrupted?"

Chapter 2

Sunday morning dawned bright and clear, the forecast called for mid-seventies and partly cloudy. The weather couldn't have been much better.

John woke up to the smell of French toast cooking in the kitchen. He lay there for a couple of minutes. "Boy, that smells good." He said under his breath.

"Honey, you better get up and eat your breakfast so we can make it to church," Anna called.

"I'll be right there!"

"You must have been really tired; it's already after 7:30."

"Wow, I didn't know I slept that late!"

He pulled on his dark blue robe and slipped his feet into slippers.

As he got to the table, Anna looked sharp in a red dress. He gave her a kiss and said, "Smells delicious, Honey!"

As he sat down, he remarked, "You look nice!"

"I bet you say that to all the girls!"

"Only the ones that serve me breakfast."

Anna shook her head, "Typical man."

"You wouldn't want any other kind."

"You're right. Sure is nice this morning."

"Yep. Beautiful. Stays this way, I can be back in the field tomorrow morning."

John took a shower and dressed while Anna worked in the kitchen.

On the way to church, John asked, "Are the kids coming over today?"

"Yep, should be here after church?"

"Tommy comin' too?"

"Said he would leave his dorm early enough to get here for lunch."

John glanced at Anna, "He find a girl at school yet?"

Anna shook her head, "No, don't think he's in any hurry."

"I sometimes wonder about that boy."

"He'll be fine. Give him time."

"I s'pose. I'll be glad to see the grandkids."

"Me too. I can't get enough of those sweet babies!"

In Sunday school class, John sat down next to Clem Adkins.

"Hey, Clem," John said, "Have you talked to Jim Rush this week?"

"No, but I heard from a couple of other guys that he's selling out and leaving the country."

John briefly described his encounter with Jim to Clem.

"Well," Clem squinted at John, "I think he's just deserting his country - the country that gave him so much. I agree with him that there's going to have to be a change here, but I think any man worth his salt ought to be willing to fight for his country."

"Fight? Not sure what you mean."

"Well, John, when the time is right, there are plenty of us who are ready and armed to have another revolution."

"I don't know, Clem..."

"Look, John, this is our home, and we gotta fight for it."

Just then, Bill the Sunday school teacher walked up to the front, "Let's start with prayer. Lord, we ask that You guide us as we study Your word."

He continued, "Let's turn to second Chronicles 7:14. Anna, would you be willing to read that for us?"

Anna found the right verse and then read, "If my people, who are called by my name, will humble themselves and pray and seek my face and turn from their wicked ways, then will I hear from heaven and will forgive their sin and will heal their land."

"Okay," Bill began, "do you think this applies to our nation today?"

Greg Bower spoke up, "I certainly think we should apply this verse. If we don't, I'm afraid of what my kids have to look forward to if we don't call on God for help."

John turned around when he heard Greg's voice. He nodded to him.

Others in the class echoed much the same sentiment. "Do you think that Christians in America today are doing this?" Bill asked.

Clem spoke up. "There's no doubt that as Christians we need to depend on God to help us. But sometimes, I think God wants us to take some matters into our own hands."

"What do you mean?" Bill asked.

"I mean our founding fathers trusted God, but they also picked up their guns and risked their lives to make sure we could live our lives the way we see best."

After the discussion, they left the room and went into the sanctuary. John looked up at the high cathedral ceiling of the old church. The sanctuary still portrayed the beautiful workmanship and ornate carvings that were there when the church was built. Light streamed through the stained glass ceilings.

John and Anna chose a pew near the middle of the sanctuary. Soon Greg and Abby sat in the same pew.

Before long the rest of the room filled with people. The service started with 'Amazing Grace' and then the congregation sang 'How Great Thou Art'.

Pastor Rick had a rousing sermon about what happens when people or nations turn their backs on God. "If we look at the history of ancient Israel, we can see that every time the people of Israel turned their backs on God, as a country, it developed major problems. When they turned back to God, God healed their land and restored them. This happened many times over hundreds of years. Eventually, though, God ran out of patience and He removed Israel as a nation until 1948."

"We as people need to be careful about the same thing. If we walk away from God, we open ourselves up to danger in our lives. The closer we walk with God, the safer we are spiritually, and the less that can harm us without God allowing it. If people turn their backs on God long enough, they run the danger of facing God's judgment, just like nations do."

After church, John turned to Greg and asked. "You and Abby are planning on bringing little Johnny over for lunch, aren't you?"

Greg laughed, "Yeah Dad, we'll bring him over and we'll come, too, if that's okay with you?"

"I'm sorry Greg, I do want to talk with you guys, too, but you know how much I enjoy seeing Johnny."

"Sure Dad, I know how we rate!"

When they got home from church, John could smell the turkey as soon as they walked through the door. Boy, did it ever smell good!

Greg and Abby got there around twelve-thirty. "Are we the first ones to make it here?" Abby asked. "Johnny sure is looking forward to playing with Samantha."

"Jeff and Sarah should be here any time now," said Anna, "They said they would be right over after their church gets out."

Sarah was John and Anna's oldest child. At 31, she was a bit older than either of the boys. She and her husband Jeff had three children. Tabitha was their oldest at ten, Thomas was seven, and little Samantha was only three.

At that point, a maroon SUV went past the side window. Three kids piled out of the back as Thomas yelled, "Grandpa, can you take me for a ride on the four-wheeler today?"

Tabitha called out, "Girls first. I want a ride, too."

Samantha chimed in, "Yeah, gools fust."

"Wait a second," exclaimed Thomas, "That's not fair, I asked first!"

Johnny ran over to Samantha and started tugging on her hand, "Play with me, Samama!"

John spoke up, "You will all get your turn on the four-wheeler, but I think we want to eat first."

As they headed toward the house, an old black VW Beetle turned into the driveway.

"Tommy's here!" said Sarah, "Still driving the first car he ever got."

In the dining room, the seven adults all sat around the antique dining table while the kids ate at a card table in the kitchen.

After thanking God for the food, John asked, "So Greg, have you had any luck finding a job yet?"

"Not anywhere near Peoria," he replied. "Oh, I could find a job as a programmer if I were willing to move halfway across the country."

"I don't want to do that," Abby crossed her arms.

Greg continued, "I've had a few odd jobs now and then, but I'd really like to find a job working with computers if possible."

Jeff replied, "I feel sorry for the guys that have to find a job right now. The economy's still tough and I'm just lucky to be able to help my Dad farm; we're up to milking about 800 cows a day now."

"Wow," John remarked, "That's a lot of work with all of the ground you guys farm too."

"Yeah, we're also farming around 2,000 acres this year."

"Did you hear about Jim Rush selling his farm? He said he plans on moving out of the country."

Jeff nodded his head, "Yeah, my dad and I have discussed buying his south farm. It's some of the best ground in the county."

"Yeah, I know it is."

"Do you know why he's leaving here?"

John shrugged, "He said that he doesn't see any future in America and he thinks we will lose everything if we stay here."

"How would that be?"

"Because of the problems here. I agree that our country has some problems, but nothing we haven't faced before."

Abby spoke up, "I know the economy has been tough for a few years, but everything I hear is that things are beginning to pick up."

"I've heard that too," Anna answered.

"If Greg could find a good job, we would be doing a lot better." Abby continued, "I'm thankful that as a nurse, I'm bringing in enough money for us to make it right now."

Tommy had been listening to the conversation and looked deep in thought. "I've looked at the numbers and things don't look good. If you think about it, the dollar doesn't actually have anything to back it, except for the fact that the Government won't let anyone put out a currency that could compete against it."

"Why is that bad?" asked Sarah.

"Well, other countries are starting to get nervous about all of the dollars that the Federal Reserve is creating and looking around for alternatives to the dollar. Did you know that the dollar has lost over 95 percent of its value since the Federal Reserve was created?"

Sarah spoke up, "I know that groceries have gone up fast over the last couple of years, but I have trouble believing that the almighty dollar could ever go away. Besides, other countries are having problems too."

Tommy replied, "Other countries have seen their currencies depreciate rapidly. In the 1920's Germany had its currency go down so fast that it took a wheelbarrow full of money to buy a loaf of bread."

"Maybe Clem's got the right idea if things get that bad," said John "Maybe we'll all need guns to keep us safe and keep looters away."

Tommy went on, "In Germany, people in the cities went out into the country and raided the farms to get food for their families."

"That's scary!" Sarah exclaimed.

"Well, if the dollar collapses, people who are dependent on the government and who live week to week will have no option but to turn to crime to get food. Think about it, wouldn't you do whatever it takes to keep your kids from starving?"

Anna spoke up, "This is kind of a depressing conversation. I know that some tough times could come, but right now we have each other and we need to be thankful for that. By the way Abby, how's the pregnancy going?"

"At my last check-up, the doctor said everything's fine. We don't want to know the sex of the baby until it's born so we're picking out both boy and girl names."

Anna's tone softened, "Abby, I don't mean to embarrass you, but if you and Greg need any help while you're off work, we can help you out." Anna gently patted her hand.

After lunch, John took the grandkids several rounds around the yard with the four-wheeler, while the other adults sat on the front porch.

When the others had left, Tommy walked over to John. "Dad, could I talk to you a minute?"

"Sure son, what is it?"

"Well, I'm not sure it's anything…"

"What do you mean?"

Tommy looked into his dad's eyes, "It's just that I hear things."

"What kind of things."

"I don't want you to worry."

"Worry about what?" John cocked his head and held out his hands.

"I suspect they may be watching you."

"Who? Why? What do you mean?"

"Well, certain parts of the government."

"Why me?" John pointed at himself.

"I suspect you're too independent-minded?"

"I don't get it?"

"I told you I didn't want to worry you." Tommy put his hand on his dad's shoulder.

"I'm confused."

"Just be aware in case anything happens."

"Not sure what you mean, but OK."

"Well, I gotta head back to school."

John gave him a quick hug, "See ya son."

After Tommy pulled out of the driveway, John and Anna went back inside. "Feels kinda empty once the kids leave, doesn't it?" John mentioned.

"Yeah, sure was good to see them."

"Wanna watch a little TV?"

"Sure, what'cha wanna watch?"

"You pick, I won't be up late."

Around 9:00, John said, "I'm heading to bed. I want to get up early to get started in the field. Night."

"Night, Honey. I'll be in before too long."

Chapter 3

The sun felt warm as it came through the window of Ken Johnson's bright red BMW. The traffic around him had come to a stop as he made his way to his office.

Ken looked thin but lean with blond hair and bright blue eyes. At 6' 2", he stood a little taller than average.

Suddenly a voice behind him yelled, "Hey Buddy, you gonna move or stay parked there?"

He took the cue and sped along the road. He turned into the parking lot and headed past the 'Homeland Security' sign. He pulled into his reserved parking spot.

As he got out of the car, he gazed at the large concrete and glass building. He went inside. There sat a heavy-set, bald officer that reminded Ken of a bulldog.

As Ken walked by, the guard greeted him, "Good morning, Mr. Johnson."

He stepped into the elevator and pushed the button for the fourth floor. As the doors opened, he turned to the right and walked to a door with his name on it.

As he opened the door, a young lady greeted him. She had long black hair, a dark tan, and a short red dress that revealed long shapely legs that ended in red high heels.

"Good morning, Mr. Johnson."

"Morning, Amanda."

"Mr. Cole wants to see you at 10:00. It sounded urgent!"

Ken stopped and gave her a puzzled look, "I wonder why he needs to see me at 10:00 o'clock on a Monday morning?"

"He didn't say. Just said to make it ASAP."

"Thank you, Amanda. Love the color of your dress!"

"Thanks, Ken."

He went into his office and closed the door. He sat at his desk and picked up the stack of memos and reports from the previous week.

At 9:50, he got up and headed out the door. He went down the well-lit hallway and took the door across from the elevator. He bounded up one flight of stairs and exited into a hallway that looked much like the one he had left.

He turned to the left and entered a door that had a sign on it, 'Alex Cole, Director'.

As he entered the office, there sat a lady who had a few gray hairs mixed in with her auburn hair. She had horn-rimmed glasses and wore a white blouse. She could have been a model for a grandmother.

The nameplate on the front of her modest desk said 'Grace Anthony'. Other than a small stack of papers and a phone to the right of it, the desk looked clean and uncluttered.

She looked up as Ken entered. "Morning, Mr. Johnson. Mr. Cole is expecting you and wants you to go on in."

"Thank you, Grace."

Ken opened the door to the inner office and stepped inside. A slightly balding man of medium height who wore a black suit with a blue tie looked up from a large ornate desk.

He stood up as Ken entered. Other than the suit being a little tight around the midsection, the man appeared to be fairly lean.

"Morning, Ken. Would you mind closing the door behind you?"

"Morning, Mr. Cole."

"Have a seat, Ken."

Ken sat on the padded chair across from the desk. He looked expectantly at the older man.

"Ken, I wanted to talk to you about something rather important. But first, can you tell me again why you decided to work with us?"

"You want the whole story?"

"Pretty much, without too much detail." Mr. Cole relaxed back in his tufted leather chair.

"Well, I grew up in New York City. My mom was a single parent and she cleaned offices at night. She barely made enough to keep the rent paid and food on the table. The fat cat capitalists she worked for never even knew she existed."

"That must have been hard for her."

"Then when I turned eleven, on her way home one night, a drunk ran a red light and broadsided her. She survived but stayed in the hospital for six months. She could never work again." Ken swallowed hard but kept his composure.

"Tough break."

"The rich guys she worked for never even sent her a get well card. They just replaced her like a piece of machinery that quit working."

"So how'd you make it through that?" Mr. Cole rested his hands behind his head,

"My mom never wanted to live on charity, but luckily, we were able to get various government assistance programs. We actually lived a little better after that, and got to spend more time with her."

"That must have had quite an impact on you."

"Yep. After seeing all the inequalities caused by capitalism, I knew I wanted to work for the government and help others get the same help we got. I soon realized that the more government we have, the more equal everyone is. I think the more government regulation we have, the better this world will be." Ken folded his arms and settled back.

"So where did you go from there?"

"I started working for the EPA right out of college. After a few years, I transferred to the NSA. I worked my way up the ranks there until a few years ago. Then you gave me a call and I've been here since."

Mr. Cole leaned forward and looked Ken the eye, "Do you like it here?"

"Yeah, I feel like I'm making a difference. May I ask where this is going?"

"I just wanted to verify what I thought about you. You are the type of person we're looking for. This Friday evening, we're having a meeting. The President of the United States will be there as well as some other VIPs. We will be discussing some important and sensitive information. After reviewing files on several prospective candidates, you've been chosen to work with us."

Ken stared at Alex for a moment. "I... I don't know what to say. I'm honored to be included."

"It will involve much of the evening on Friday and we will have a car at your place to pick you up at 7:30 sharp. Can I count on you? I believe this is the biggest opportunity of your lifetime."

Without hesitation, Ken replied, "Yes sir, I'll be ready."

"Good, I assured them you could make it. I don't need to tell you that everything about the evening must be kept top secret. I'm sure you understand."

"Yes, I figured that."

Ken spent the rest of the day preparing reports, but his mind had trouble staying on his work.

He went home to his apartment after work. At 7:25, he headed back down by the front door.

"Good evening, Mr. Johnson," the doorman greeted him, "Will you be going out this evening?"

"Yes, a car will be here for me soon."

"Have a good evening."

"Thank you!"

Promptly at 7:30, a long black limousine pulled up at the front door. The driver got out and opened the door. "Mr. Johnson, I presume?"

"Yes."

Ken got in the back seat. As soon as the door closed, he noticed that the windows were tinted from both sides. The passenger compartment remained dark except for a small dome light that stayed on.He rode in silence for nearly half an hour. When the car finally stopped, he heard the driver get out and come around to open his door. Upon stepping out, he saw the entrance to a huge stone mansion.

On either side of the doorway were two large men in suits. They weren't talking but kept an eye on everyone that exited from the limousines as they pulled upAs he made his way to the entrance, he looked around. It appeared they were in a wooded area, and he could just make out the outlines of guards where the driveway emerged from the woods. Even from this distance, he could tell they were armed.

"Boy, the security is tight here," he said under his breath. He had no idea if they were somewhere still in the city or on the outskirts. As soon as he went through the massive doorway, a butler greeted him. "Good evening, Mr. Johnson, please follow me.

He led Ken through a wide hallway to an expansive room. Although the room had large chandeliers, it was anything but bright, with floor to ceiling paneling stained to a dark walnut color. In the center of the room stood the largest table Ken had ever seen. There were upholstered wood chairs around the table and most of them were occupied.

The butler led him to a chair near the end of the table. As he looked around, he recognized Alex right across from him. Near the head of the table sat the President of the United States. A few other faces he recognized from pictures. Some of these people were the richest in the world! Many of the faces, he had no idea who they were.

The other seats filled quickly. As they were filling, servants brought drinks and hors d'oeuvres around to everyone seated there. It surprised him to find that they brought him mineral water and a fruit salad.

"Hey, Alex," he whispered, "how did they know I don't drink alcohol and I'm a vegetarian?"

"They know. Don't question too much."

Promptly at 8:30, an immaculately manicured man in a black tux came in and took a seat at the head of the table. As soon as he took a seat, the servants hastily left the room and shut the doors.

The man began, "We're here to update everyone on the progress of the plan and to resolve any difficulties that anyone may be having. For those of you who are new here, I'm sure that it goes without saying that nothing discussed here goes out of this room. You don't even tell your family. This is for their protection. Does everyone understand?" His voice completely lacked emotion. It sounded icy; it had no hatred nor warmth.

After an awkward pause, while the man looked around the room, Ken and three others mumbled an affirmative.

"Good," replied the man in charge. "Now we'll brief you on the plan and any updates we have. We've been well aware for many decades that the current system that we have in this country and others is extremely inefficient and unfair to the majority. There is not enough order to it and no planning."

"Some people practically starve, while others live in incredible abundance. Natural resources are exploited and used to pollute the planet. We intend to create a society where things are planned centrally and resources are allocated fairly. People will truly be equal in such a society. People will be assigned to work where they are best suited to work. With this type of central planning, our society can rise to a greatness not seen in history. The Mayans had a similar system and they achieved incredible feats for the technology they had at the time."

"With our technology, we can achieve incredible things with everyone working toward the same goal. The only obstacle in our way at this time is that the current system is viewed as working. This will not last long. We've been working for decades to get this country in a position to be ready for change."

He paused and looked around the room. "In order to achieve our goals, we had to first destroy the existing system. This has been relatively easy to accomplish. Simply by promising people that the government is the answer to all of their problems, they have expected the government to give them more and more.

"Because of this, we now have the system so overloaded that it's only a matter of time until we can engineer a crisis that will bring it all down. When that happens, we have most of the pieces in place to restore order. It will be inevitable that some casualties will occur, but we have to keep our eye on the goal. The resulting society will be the greatest society ever created and you will be part of the plan.

"Now let's get down to business. Mr. President, we've been most impressed with your progress so far. How is everything going with getting the forces in place when it comes time to restore order?"

President Burke stood and responded, "It's progressing quite nicely at this point. We are not 100% ready yet, but we're much closer. The military is slowly being changed to be willing to do whatever is necessary to keep the peace. I've succeeded in building an internal peacekeeping force that's almost as well-armed and powerful as the military. As always, all of these things have been done gradually so as not to raise an alarm and create rebellion against the government."

Then the man looked at Alex. "Mr. Cole, how are things at homeland security? I do believe that is one of the best moves we've made in recent years. Creating Homeland Security has greatly helped with the ability to control the population in the future."

"Well, sir," Alex began. "I believe we are making excellent progress. We've been stocking up on both weapons and ammunition for quite some time. The public may get a little alarmed when they first hear about a large ammunition purchase, but they soon get on with their lives and forget about it after a while. We're also poised to control much of the nation and to be the focal point for all other agencies to be centrally managed."

"I see you have a recruit that has passed all of our examinations. I assume his ideologies line up with ours?"

"Yes, sir," Alex agreed. "He's a firm believer in central planning and having a largely government-controlled society."

"Very well," the man responded. After checking on the progress of five or six others, the man said, "It appears things are progressing well. It will not be long until this plan will come to fruition. We won't meet again for the next year. I'll be in contact with you if there's a specific action I need you to take."

With that, he rose and exited the room, signaling the end of the meeting. Alex went over to him. "Ken, could I talk with you for a minute?"

"Sure, Alex, what's up?"

"First of all, what did you think?"

"It felt a little overwhelming."

Alex pulled up a chair beside him, "It felt that way for me the first time I got invited here too."

"So, what role do I play in all this?"

"Well, I'm grooming you to be a possible replacement for heading up our Midwest division."

Ken arched his eyebrows, "What do you mean by replacement?"

"The guy that's ready for that position now is creating some concerns."

"What kind of concerns?"

"Can't go into detail now, but we want you to be ready." Alex patted Ken's shoulder.

"What should I be doing to get ready?"

"Familiarize yourself with our concerns in the area."

"Like what?"

Alex reached into his briefcase. "Here's a file for example on a farmer in the area."

"What's he done?"

"Nothing really, but we have information on him and we know how he thinks."

"I don't understand. Is thinking wrong?"

Alex took a deep breath. "No, but his type could create problems."

"How's that?"

"He's independent-minded and has a strong sense of right and wrong."

"That's a problem?" Ken cocked his head.

"Could be. Those types will rebel against the government if they think the government is wrong."

"I see now why he could be a problem."

"I'm glad you understand."

Ken held out his hand. "Can I see his file?"

"Sure, here it is."

"What's his name?"

"His name is John Bower."

Chapter 4

On Thanksgiving Day that year, the day dawned bright and clear but cool. Anna started preparing lunch by 7:30 that morning.

"Smelling that turkey sure makes me hungry!" John exclaimed as he came through the kitchen.

"If you're too hungry, eat something to hold you over."

"Don't mind if I do. Lunch at noon?"

"Yep, everybody should be here by then."

At 11:30, Jeff and Sarah pulled into the driveway. John greeted them at the door and took their jackets.

"Sure does smell good in here, Mom!" Sarah yelled at the kitchen.

"I'm hungry!" shouted Thomas

"Me too, little buddy," said John.

"Here comes Greg and Abby," Sarah mentioned.

Anna called from the kitchen, "I can't wait to hold little Jenny again!"

Sarah responded, "Me first! I haven't seen her since she was born - two weeks ago already!"

"Girls, girls, don't fight over the baby!" Jeff joked.

Greg came in the door carrying a basket with a baby blanket over it. Abby followed behind with Johnny on her heels.

Anna came out of the kitchen and pulled back the blanket. "She sure looks a lot like you, Abby."

"That's what they say," Abby glowed.

"Pretty like her mother," mentioned Greg.

"You're just saying that to win points with me."

"No, I mean it!"

"Sure, except for the extra weight I gained."

"You still look good."

Sarah picked up Jenny, "Hey, pretty little lady."

Just then the door opened. Tommy stepped into the room.

"Hey, Tommy's here. Now we can eat!" Jeff rubbed his stomach.

"I'm glad somebody noticed me," Tommy said.

"Oh, we're not excited about you, we're just hungry." Jeff answered.

"Oh thanks, I know how I rate."

"Time to get to the table!" Anna commanded.

After the blessing, as they were passing the dishes, John's dad asked him, "John, did you have a good year farming?"

"Yeah, it was okay," replied John, "I wondered about the start of the year. I thought it would never warm up."

"I know. Me too. "

"I would say that we're rather fortunate to do as well as we do. It seems like it takes a lot more to live these days."

Greg spoke up, "I agree with you there. I get odd jobs and work part-time at the lumber yard."

Abby joined in, "I still don't know how we would make ends meet if you and Mom didn't share from your garden and the beef that you butchered."

"We're glad we can help you out," said Anna. "You just take good care of our little granddaughter."

Abby continued, "Yeah, groceries do seem a lot higher this year. Another thing I noticed is that on some things, the packages are smaller."

"Well it's not that stuff is higher, but the dollar's worth less," said Tommy.

Jeff broke into the conversation, "What makes it harder for farmers like my dad and me is that there's so much government regulation."

"That's true," replied Tommy

Jeff added, "We seem to spend way too much time filling out all of the paperwork required to run a big farm. With employees and all, I wish we could just farm and not have to file so much stuff with the government."

"I'm afraid that's part of the deal to farm today," said John. "You should try the documentation required to be listed as certified organic."

"That's part of the reason we've never tried it."

"Changing the subject a little," continued John, "I got an email from Jim Rush the other day. He bought a farm in South America and he sent me his address and contact info. He said that a lot less red tape is required to farm there."

"You planning on moving there too?" asked John's dad.

"No," replied John. "But if Anna and I ever got time to travel, it might be fun to visit someone in a foreign country. I kept his info just in case."

After dinner, the adults were relaxing in the family room while the kids went upstairs to play.

"Tommy," said Jeff, "you're up on current events most of the time. What do you think is going to happen with our economy? Is there a good way out of this?"

"Well," began Tommy, "I don't think that anyone in leadership in this country wants to fix the problem. Our government is going in debt faster than ever and they're already over their head with debt."

"Ain't that the truth?!"

"If it weren't for the Federal Reserve creating money at record-breaking speed and then loaning it to the government, we would have already hit a wall."

Jeff paused for a moment, "Won't we do something before it gets that far?"

"The problem is that most people don't seem to know or care. As long as things don't change too much, people just keep going on with their lives and pretend there isn't a problem."

"Will our government do something about it?"

"It seems like those in charge want to see the economy crash. I think it's only a matter of time until we have a major crisis."

"Maybe Clem has the right idea," John said. "Maybe we do need another American revolution to take this country back."

"I'm not sure that'll work this time," replied Tommy. "If the dollar collapses, people will turn to crime in droves. It'll be complete chaos with everyone out for himself. If the government comes in to restore order, I think most people will welcome it. I just don't think people have the stomach to handle a full out war."

Greg spoke up. "I've heard that the government is arming up and are buying a lot of hollow-point ammunition. It seems strange when even the Social Security office buys a bunch of ammunition."

"Even the local police are buying a lot more weapons than they used to have," Sarah said.

"Yeah, it seems weird that they need so much firepower with the low rate of crime that we have here. I know crime is rising in Chicago and other big cities, but in small communities, I don't see the need for the police to be so heavily armed."

Anna interjected, "Maybe it's a sign of the end times. We know from reading the Bible that times will get worse, just before the end."

"You may be right, Mom," said Tommy, "But it's hard to know if we're just going through a change like countries have throughout history, or if it really is near the end."

"I'm concerned for the kids growing up today."

"Yeah, I'm worried about my kid's future!" Sarah exclaimed.

"Things were simpler when we were kids," Anna said.

"I do know that this is not anywhere near the country that you and Dad grew up in. The government's not going to let go of any control easily. In fact, they're seizing power at an alarming rate." Tommy continued.

Greg spoke up, "I think it's scary."

"I could easily see the government nationalizing all businesses and farms if we have an economic collapse. They would just about have to in order to feed everyone."

Abby erupted, "This is so depressing! I'm afraid for my kids trying to grow up in this kind of world. Can we change the subject?"

"Yeah," John agreed, "Are we still having our family Christmas at noon on Christmas day? Can everybody make it?"

"Tommy, will your wife be able to come?" teased Sarah.

Tommy replied, "I thought she was coming with you, Sarah. I kind of hoped that would be your Christmas present to me."

Everybody had a good laugh at that.

After dinner, John's dad pulled him aside and asked to speak with him in the garage.

"What's up, Dad? You seem not quite yourself today." John asked.

"It's your mother." his dad sighed. "I'm concerned about her. She hasn't felt well for about three weeks now. I didn't want to say anything at the table because I didn't want to worry everyone. I thought you ought to know what's happening though."

John's face showed his concern. "Does she know what it is? Has she been to the doctor?"

"Well, you know your mom. She's stubborn and keeps insisting that she'll feel better soon. She did tell me she would go to the doctor after Thanksgiving if she didn't feel better."

John put his hand on his dad's shoulder. "Yeah, since Anna's parents were killed in that car wreck 25 years ago, I'd hate to see her worry about losing her mother-in-law too. I know how close they are.

Chapter 5

As they gathered around the dinner table on Christmas day, the smell of roast duck filled the air.

Right after the blessing, John asked, "Sorry to bring up the elephant in the room. But Mom, how are you feeling about your oncologist's treatment plan?"

"Well, you know they're going to give me chemo and radiation, but it's OK, I trust in God's perfect plan."

"Well, we're gonna keep praying for you."

Anna spoke up, "You know we all love you."

"Let's have a good time together and remember that I'm not dead yet!" she quipped. "Christmas is a time of celebration. Let's keep it that way this year."

After a few more jokes, the tone lightened up.

Greg announced, "I've started getting a few jobs freelancing on the Internet. I figured if I couldn't get a full-time job as a programmer, I might as well do some freelancing. It helps a lot with the budget. Plus Abby is back to work, so it makes things a lot easier."

"That's great!" said Anna. "I just want to say that I'm so thankful for our family this year. I want you to know that every one of you has a special place in my heart!"

"Thanks, Mom," said Sarah. "I have to admit that the older I get, the more I appreciate family."

"I agree with you, Honey," said Jeff. "I remember when I was a kid, Christmas meant lots of presents. Now, all that matters to me is to be able to get together with my family."

"That reminds me! We have to leave by 4:00 to get to your family Christmas tonight."

After lunch, they all gathered in the family room around a tree that overflowed with gifts. It looked like it floated on a sea of presents.

After singing some Christmas carols, Thomas asked, "Is it time yet? Can we open presents now? Can I pass them out?"

"Slow down there little man," laughed Jeff, "I suppose it's time to start the presents. All of the kids can help pass them out. Thomas, why don't you and Tabitha help Samantha and Johnny pass out the gifts?"

"Presents!" Samantha said.

"Goody, goody!" chimed in Johnny.

It didn't take long before the living room looked like a paper mill had blown up in the middle of it. After several paper ball fights, John got out a couple of large trash bags and the adults cleaned up the floor.

Four o'clock came quickly and Jeff and Sarah left with their family. Johnny played with his new train set in the middle of the living room. Jenny slept soundly in the den.

The adults lounged around the living room with some of them half asleep from all of the food and relaxation.

"Tommy," Greg said. "I read the other day that some countries are thinking about not using the U.S. dollar when they trade with each other. Do you know anything about that?"

"Actually, that's kind of old news, Greg," replied Tommy, "China has phased out using our dollar whenever they can. They prefer to use their own currency."

"I can understand why."

"Russia is moving away from using the dollar too. They use it only when they trade with us or with a few of our closest allies. The International Monetary Fund is issuing Special Drawing Rights based on several currencies for countries to use for trading."

"So, what's wrong with that?"

"Well, the whole situation has me worried. I am afraid that the dollar could lose its position as the world currency quickly," continued Tommy.

"Why is that so bad?" asked Abby. "What's so bad about other countries trading with other currencies?"

"Well," began Tommy, "there are way too many dollars out there. If the rest of the world doesn't use them, then they will all come back here to this country."

"What's so bad about that?" asked Abby. "If that happens, we'll all be a lot richer because there are more dollars to go around."

"That's true," said Tommy, "but when there are a lot more dollars and the same amount of stuff, everything will cost a lot more. That's how you get inflation."

Greg looked at him. "Don't we always have inflation?"

"Yeah, but if you get too many dollars all at once, you can get hyper-inflation and things can get so out of control that people won't even want dollars anymore."

"I think I understand that," remarked Greg. "If the whole driveway were covered with diamonds instead of stones, then diamonds wouldn't be worth much. It goes the same for money."

"You've got it," said Tommy. "The worst part is that dollars have no use except as currency. There have been times of hyperinflation when people would paper their walls with paper money because it became so worthless."

John spoke up, "Changing the subject, Mom, since only the adults are here, what else are the doctors saying?"

"Well, doctors only give statistics," she scoffed. "They say I've got about a 35% chance."

"Oh, Mom!" exclaimed Anna.

"Now, it's not as bad as that. I still feel pretty good."

John looked at his mom, "I think you're looking good, Mom."

"Thank you, Son."

"How are you doing, Dad?"

Tears welled up in his dad's eyes, "I'm - holding up."

John's mom reached over and took his hand. "We're looking on the positive side. We're all terminal you know."

"Why do we always have to talk about such depressing stuff when we get together?" asked Anna. "Let's just have a good time for Christmas. We need to cherish every moment we have together as a family."

After that, the conversation moved to small talk until about seven when Greg and Abby took the kids home to put them to bed. John's mom felt tired, so she and John's dad left then too.

Tommy slept in his old room that night. John and Anna relaxed the rest of the evening, but John could tell that Anna appeared concerned about something.

Finally, he asked her point-blank, "Anna, you seem to be not yourself tonight. Is there something wrong?"

"Oh, it's your mom, John. I can't help but think that this may be the last Christmas we have with her."

"Oh, Honey, don't worry so much."

"What if I'm right?"

"We'll face that when it comes."

Chapter 6

On January 10th, John ran some errands in town. When he got back to the house, Anna spoke up, "That took longer than I expected, was there a problem?"

John smiled at her, "I stopped by Mom and Dad's house on the way. Mom looks really good."

"That's great!"

"Yeah, she said she feels good too. The tumor has shrunk considerably."

"That's so encouraging."

Two days later, John and Anna were eating dinner when the phone rang.

"I'll get it," said John.

He picked up the phone, "Hello? ... Oh, hi Dad, ... We're good, how's Mom? ... Great! ... Yeah, Dad, ... You're gonna do what? ... Yeah, I s'pose so, ... Ok, have a good time and be careful, ... Bye."

He went back to the table. Anna looked at him, "What was that all about?"

John stared at her for a second, and then smirked, "Dad and Mom are going to Cancun for a week."

"Really? When?"

"They're leaving Friday."

"What brought that on?"

John took a deep breath, "Mom's been feeling good and Dad wants to make memories while they can."

"I guess I can understand that."

"I hope they have a great time." He took Anna's hand.

"Me too. Do they need a ride to the airport?"

"Nah, I think Dad will drive."

Late in January, highs were in the teens. The sun reflected off the snow. The whole family came to the house for Sunday dinner again. John's parents looked healthy with their light tan.

John turned to his dad. "So, Dad, how was Cancun?"

"Yeah," Abby said, "Tell us all the details."

"It was a great choice."

John's mom chimed in, "It was incredible!"

Anna looked at her. "Tell us about it."

"We ate some great seafood. We walked on the beach and felt the warm breeze. It felt like a honeymoon all over again."

John's dad looked warmly at her, "I can't remember you looking more beautiful."

She smiled at him, "I spent time with the love of my life."

John grinned, "Maybe you two lovebirds need your privacy. It's gettin' kinda mushy in here."

Everybody laughed.

Anna said, "Got any pictures?"

John's mom pulled out her phone. "Gather 'round kids and I'll show you some beautiful pictures - and some video of two old people trying to dance."

John and Anna watched through the kitchen window as his parents left that afternoon. They walked holding hands till they got to the car. Then John's dad held the door as his mom got in.

Anna had a tear in her eye. "They have so much love for each other!"

John responded, "Yeah, hopefully they'll have a lot of years together yet."

"Your mom looked so good today."

———

Nearly two weeks later the phone rang again. Anna answered. "Hello, … Oh, hi Dad, how's Mom? … Oh - oh, no! … Of course, we'll be right there!"

John looked at her with a concerned look on his face. "What happened?"

"Your mom got sick. They're at the hospital now. I told your dad we'd be right there.

John and Anna got in the car and headed to the hospital. When they got there, they found John's dad.

John spoke first. "What's up, Dad?"

"I'm afraid the cancer's back. She just suddenly started throwing up."

"What did the doctor say?"

His voice broke, "He said she may only have a few weeks!"

John held his dad while Anna took his hand.

She passed away by early March. The funeral hit the whole family hard, but John had never seen his dad look so old and worn out.

After the funeral, he and Anna went home.

"Are you OK, Honey?" asked Anna.

"Yeah, I just thought about my parents."

"Bout what?"

John shook his head, "They were married for close to 60 years."

"That's a long time."

"Never seen my Dad look so old."

Anna took his hand. "It's gotta be tough on him."

"Don't know how I would make it if I lost you."

"You're tough. You'd be OK."

John paused for a moment, "I don't know…"

"Something else bothering you?"

"I don't know, It just seems like…"

Anna looked him in the eyes, "Like what?"

"Like nothin's going to be the same again. Like things are gonna turn bad."

"What do you mean?"

"I just sense that we might be in for hard times."

Anna moved close to him with concern in her eyes.
"Why is that?"

"Gas is over $4 a gallon and other prices seem higher."

"I agree."

"Something just doesn't feel right."

Chapter 7

Abdul Quadeer Ahmed had been born in Lebanon. He grew up in a devout Muslim family and had studied the Quran all of his life.

By the time he was 15, he knew that he would be destined to die for Allah at some time in his life. He knew he had been chosen for a special purpose.

Now he was 30 years old and lived in Chicago. He had a good job delivering packages and lived in a decent neighborhood in Old Town. He liked being near downtown and liked the hustle and bustle of the city.

Ten years before, he had come across the border from Mexico. He and three other guys from his town were able to get across the border carrying large backpacks without too much trouble. After they were about ten miles into California, they were met by a contact that had been prearranged.

All three of them were comfortably settled in the Chicago area. They all received papers and were able to get driver's licenses and other necessary paperwork. They seldom met together except when they went to the mosque.

Four years ago, Abdul had met Ashley. With her small but curvy frame, she looked quite attractive. She had light brown hair that framed out her pretty face. Ashley claimed to be a Christian, but she only went to church sporadically. She fell in love with Abdul's charming personality and his dark complexion and brown eyes.

After dating for about six months, they decided to get married. Abdul insisted they have a Muslim wedding. Ashley figured that Allah is just the name that Abdul called God, so she felt fine with incorporating Abdul's religion into their lives.

Abdul seemed always charming but seldom opened up fully to Ashley. He stood firm about being in charge of the household though. However, one room in the basement he kept locked at all times. He told Ashley that it is his man cave and he felt like it would violate the sanctity of his cave if she were allowed into it.

Eight months after they were married, Abdul came home to find the table set and candles lighting the dining room.

He took his usual seat and expressed curiosity about what was going on. Ashley came out of the kitchen with a big smile on her face. "We're celebrating tonight, Honey!"

Abdul seemed really puzzled now. "Just what are we celebrating my love?"

"We're celebrating the growth of our family," she responded. "I'm pregnant!"

He pretended to be excited. "That's great! What shall we name him?"

Ashley looked at him, "How do you know it is going to be a 'him'? It just as well might be a girl."

"Allah will allow me to have a son to carry on my name."

He proved to be right. They had a boy. Over the next few years, they had two more boys.

"Now that we have a family, I want all of us to go to the mosque together," Abdul mentioned to her one day.

"How about we go to a church some weekends so the boys can see both ways to God?"

Abduls face darkened. "No, I am the man of the house. We will go to the mosque."

"But I think they should see both ways."

"No. We will do as I say. That's all."

The look on his face told Ashley there would be no more discussion.

Every once in a while, someone that Ashley didn't know came to the house carrying a package of some sort. At times like this, Abdul would take them into his man cave for a while. Soon they would emerge, and the visitor would leave without saying anything to her.

One time after they left, Ashley asked, "What are they always bringing here?"

"It's something I'm working on."

"Well, what is it?"

"It's an idea I have to free me from my job."

Ashley looked hurt, "Why can't I see it?"

"It's a surprise, I want to keep it a secret."

"You act like it's a national secret."

He gave her a charming smile. "If you saw it, I'd have to kill you."

"OK, so you won't tell me. I get it."

As time went on, she began to wonder more and more about what he worked on in the basement, but he always kept the key on him and would never tell her anymore about it.

Ashley developed a friendship with the lady next door. She had met her unexpectedly one day when they were both leaving at the same time and Ashley's car wouldn't start.

"Car problems?"

"Yeah" Ashley replied. "I just wanted to go to the grocery store for a few things for dinner."

"Why don't you ride with me? I am going there too."

Ashley flashed a brilliant smile, "Thank you! Is there room for my boys?"

"Sure, my vans big enough. Name's Linda, what's yours?"

"I'm Ashley. I really appreciate this."

Linda had two little girls and she and Ashley spent a lot of time together on Ashley's days off. It helped to have someone that Ashley could open up to.

"Linda, how do you and Dave seem to get along so well?" Ashley asked her one day.

"Well, we both trust God to work out our differences."

"That seems a little simplistic to me."

"I know, but it's the truth."

Ashley stared at her for a few seconds, "I sometimes wish Abdul and I could do that."

"Marriage is a lot of work."

"Tell me about it. Sometimes I feel like Abdul doesn't view me as an equal."

Linda turned toward Ashley, "He's good to you though isn't he?"

"Yeah, he treats me well, but…."

"But, what?"

Ashley sighed, "I feel like I'm a child or a toy to him."

"It could be the way his culture is."

"I suppose. We don't have a bad marriage, just not the best."

Linda nodded, "We all feel that way at times."

"I s'pose. He is a good man over-all."

Chapter 8

On June 3rd, John got a visit from the police. "Are you John Bower?" the officer asked.

"Yes, I am. Is something wrong?"

"We need you to come down to the hospital," the officer said. "I'm sorry, but we need you to identify a body. We believe it's your father. Someone found him dead in his car in the Walmart parking lot. It appears he had a heart attack."

"Anna!" John called. "Could you come here?"

"Coming, Dear!"

As she came around the corner and saw his face, she asked, "What's wrong?"

"This officer just told me we need to identify a body. They think it's Dad."

Her face lightened a shade. "Oh no, what happened?"

"They found him at Walmart. They think he had a heart attack."

At the hospital, John looked at the old man lying on the table. With the gray stubble and the lines on his face, he looked small and quite old.

John stood for a few minutes looking at the still body. "Yeah, that's Dad." Under his breath added, "He looks older than I remembered."

Anna put her hand on his arm.

John wiped tears from his eyes. "He just didn't seem to have much desire to live after Mom passed away."

"I know, Honey."

"I suppose he's better off now."

John and Anna made the funeral arrangements. Pastor Rick did the funeral. As John listened, he reached over and took Anna's hand.

She looked at him and gave his hand a squeeze.

After the service, they all filed into the dining area of the church. John sat beside Tommy.

"The job I had last year with the maintenance department at college isn't available this summer," said Tommy. "I suppose I'll need to find another summer job."

"Tommy," replied John, "I've been thinking about getting help for the farm. Why don't you just come home for the summer? I could pay you instead and you could have free room and board."

"Yeah, I think I'd like that," replied Tommy. "Besides, I can't get any food at college that's half as good as Mom's."

That weekend, John took his pickup to the college to help Tommy move home for the summer.

When they walked into the house, Anna greeted them. "Tommy, I'm so glad you're home for the summer. The house seemed so empty with just me and your dad."

"Glad to be home, Mom."

"Your room is all ready for you."

"Thanks."

That evening at dinner Anna remarked, "I can't believe how much groceries have gone up. I think I have to pay at least ten to twenty percent more for the same stuff that I bought last fall."

John nodded."Yeah, I know. I've seen a lot of price increases in fuel and supplies for the farm."

"These prices are getting ridiculous."

"I agree. You know Anna, those CD's we have are coming due this week. I hate to reinvest them at less than one percent when that money buys less and less all of the time."

Anna stood and picked up the dirty plates. "Yeah, it just doesn't make sense."

"What do you think of pulling the money out of the bank and buying some silver and gold with it?"

"Whatever you think. I agree that if we leave it in cash, it just seems to be losing value."

She took the plates to the dishwasher, "What do you think Tommy?"

"I think that's a smart move. I would consider buying some silver coins in case the time ever gets here when you need them for barter," said Tommy.

"What do you think is behind all of this inflation, Tommy?" John asked.

"Well, as I've mentioned before, the Federal Reserve has created too much money. They did this to help the government and the housing market incur more debt. Basically, they created money and bought up all of the debt they would create. This kept interest rates down so we could afford this debt."

John hesitated, then looked at Tommy, "Why didn't we have more inflation before this?"

"Well, we got by with this for so long because other countries used our dollars for trading with each other."

John picked up the leftover chicken. "What difference did that make?"

"The world had a huge demand for those dollars. But, now other countries like China and Russia are using their own money to trade with each other and a lot of smaller countries are going along with them."

John opened the fridge. "How does that affect us?"

"All of those extra dollars have nowhere to go, except back here in the U.S. With all of those extra dollars coming home, they go down in value and it looks like everything else is going up."

John sat back down. "Has this happened anywhere else?"

"Yeah, the same thing happened in Germany in the 1920s. The problem is that it becomes a vicious circle. The more our dollar goes down, the less other countries want it. The fewer dollars they use, the more they go down in value."

"Is there anything we can do to stop it?"

Tommy shook his head. "I don't see how. There have already been too many dollars created. Often there's a lag of several years between when money is created and when people start to feel the effects of it. Besides, our country is too addicted to borrowed money and nobody will make the hard decisions they need to make."

After supper, John went to the computer and checked the prices of gold and silver coins online. "Whoa! These have gone up a lot in the last few months!"

"People go for precious metals in uncertain times," mentioned Tommy.

Three weeks later, the three of them were having supper again when Greg called. Anna answered the phone. "Hey, I've got great news Mom! I got a job as a computer programmer and it pays just about half again as much as I hoped for."

"That's great! When do you start?"

"I get to start Monday. It's only a 20 minutes' drive from here. This is a real answer to prayer."

Anna turned toward the table. "Hey John, Greg got a job!"

"Congratulations Greg!" yelled John.

A few days later, Anna came home from the store. "John, I filled up the car today and gas is over $5 per gallon. I've never seen gas that high before."

"Yeah, I heard about that. Thankfully, the price of crops is going up too. That's the only way I can afford to farm anymore."

Anna snorted, "With the price of stuff, we may have to eat your crops."

John nodded, "You may be right!" He looked at Tommy. "By the way, I'm going to Chicago tomorrow to buy some silver and gold coins. I think I found a dealer I can trust. Tommy, do you want to go with me?"

"Sure Dad, it's been a while since I've been to the Windy City. I'd be glad to go with you and help you find your way around."

"Oh thanks, Tommy. Don't know how I've made it so long without your guidance."

"No problem, Dad. I'll be glad to tell you where to go whenever I need to."

"Boys, boys," Anna chimed in, "You both better get to bed early tonight so you can get a good start in the morning."

"I'm fine with that," replied John, "But what's for dinner. I can't sleep on an empty stomach."

The next morning, John and Tommy climbed into the red Chevy pickup and left around 5:00 in the morning. Anna had packed some fried egg sandwiches for their breakfast.

They arrived at the coin dealer as it opened. The store was a small block building in a strip mall. About half the mall appeared vacant.

They went inside and looked around. There were antique coins of all types, as well as gold and silver bars. Everything was locked behind glass cases.

The sign behind the counter said, "Due to the high cost of ammo, no warning shots will be fired."
Next to it, a sign read, "You loot, we shoot."

Behind the counter stood an older man with a goatee and a handlebar mustache. "May I help you, gentlemen?"

"We're wanting to buy some gold and silver coins that will hold their value and could be used for barter if need be," John said.

"We have some great options for you. You're probably not looking for highly collectible coins, but something that you can buy for the price of the metal in them."

He showed them several options. In about half an hour, John and Tommy made their choices. The man totaled everything up.

"Wow," said John, "That's a bit more than I expected."

"Yeah, prices are only going up now. But it sure beats leaving your money in the bank."

"I suppose you're right about that."

John paid the man in cash. Then he and Tommy carried their purchases to the truck. They placed them under the seat and got in the truck.

After they got home, John put the bags in the bottom of the freezer in his shop.

That Sunday, the whole family came over for lunch again.

During lunch, Jeff mentioned, "I'm not sure what's going on, but it seems like all of our help got jobs elsewhere. They're getting paid a lot more than we used to pay too. Dad, you're lucky that Tommy is helping you this year."

"I've heard that from other farmers too," John said. "It just seems like the economy is going full tilt."

"Yeah, everybody's working and spending money. I don't get it. I thought with prices getting higher all the time, it would be a bad thing and keep people from buying as much."

John looked at Tommy, "Tommy, how does that fit in with your theory of the country being in trouble. Unemployment is below three percent now. That means it's practically nonexistent right now."

"The same thing happened in the Weimar Republic in the 1920s," said Tommy. "What happens is that when money depreciates so fast, money comes out of savings and goes into goods. People figure they are losing less money if they own things than if their money is in the bank."

John's face lightened, "Like we took our money out of CDs."

"Right, all kinds of money is coming out of savings and going into goods. That's why everybody is working. They have to produce more goods and sell them. "

"So isn't that a good thing?"

"The problem is that the more money that comes out of savings, the more the value of money will drop."

"How's your job going, Greg?" Sarah said, changing the subject. "We're so excited that you were able to get a good job."

"It's going fantastic!" said Greg. "It's great to be working in the field that I went to college for. They've already given me a raise. I 've never made this much money in my life!"

"I'm so glad for you!" exclaimed Anna. "It seems like it's been forever that you've been looking for a job like this."

Near the middle of August, John got a letter from his banker. "Hey Anna, this letter says they're raising the rate on our farm loan 3 percent!"

"Why's that? We've always paid on time!"

"I know, I'm just glad we don't owe much."

"I'm concerned for those who owe a lot on their farms."

"Well, as high as the price of crops is, they'll probably be OK."

He went upstairs and knocked on Tommy's bedroom door. "Hey, Tommy, ya got a minute?"

Tommy opened the door, "Sure, Dad, what'cha need?"

John held up the letter. "This letter says my interest rates are going up 3%. How's that fit in your theory of the dollar depreciating? Isn't the government trying to keep interest rates down?"

"I just got an email about that from an investment guy. Here, I'll show it to you."

John followed Tommy over to his computer. In just a few clicks, Tommy had it opened up.

"See, Dad, right here he says that as the dollar devalues, interest rates will have to rise or no one would lend dollars. Investors have to find the rates attractive."

"That makes sense. I guess I wouldn't keep my money in dollars either unless I were getting a high rate of return."

"Also, if rates stayed low, people would borrow all they could and invest in land or something that didn't go down in value so fast."

"That's true. I could do that, but I'm worried about what will happen in this crazy economy. I've never seen anything like it."

Near the end of August, John got a call. He happened to be home for lunch. "Hello?" pause, "This is John Bower." Another long pause. "Again? You guys just raised my rate a couple of weeks ago!" After about thirty seconds, "I guess I understand. I'm not sure what's happening either."

"What was that about?" asked Anna.

"They're raising my rates again,"

"How come?"

John sat back down at the table. "Same reason as before."

"This is getting ridiculous."

"I agree."

"Prices are still going crazy too. I'm scared, John."

John sighed, "Me too. Maybe Tommy's right about all this."

Tommy spoke up, "I honestly hope I'm not."

In Sunday school that weekend, John sat beside Clem Adkins. "Things are getting kind of crazy out there with prices and interest rates going up so fast."

"I agree," said Clem. "I think it's part of a conspiracy on the part of some very powerful people. However, there are a lot of good people in this country who won't stand for it."

"Well, what can we do?"

"There's a large group of us who are preparing for another revolution. You really should get a couple of assault rifles and join with us, John. We're ready for this."

"I don't know - I don't think I'm prepared to shoot anybody. I'm not sure I could actually fire on fellow Americans if it came right down to it."

Clem looked John in the eyes and pointed at him, "Your family's freedom and lives may depend on it."

During the church service, John appeared lost in thought for a few minutes. Soon though, he turned his focus to Pastor Rick. He preached from the book of Revelation. "One thing about the end time prophecies that disturbs me is that I cannot find any mention of a country that closely resembles the United States. If we were a small nation, I could understand that. However, we are the greatest superpower the world has known. It just seems strange that we wouldn't be mentioned in a major worldwide conflict."

When Pastor Rick finished the sermon, John again appeared deep in thought.

After church, the family all came over for lunch. Little Jenny captured a lot of attention. She walked around and repeatedly said "Mama". She laughed a lot and caused everyone else to laugh with her.

Samantha and Johnny were fighting over their toys. John came over to them and knelt down. "Hey you two, if you quit fighting, I'll get the four-wheeler out after we eat."

They both started playing together amicably and much more quietly.

Sarah mentioned, "Jeff and I have an anniversary coming up next week. I want him to take me to Chicago and stay at a fancy hotel and maybe go see a live show."

"Oh, that would be fun!" said Anna.

"Yeah, but he doesn't seem to want to. I know we have the money. Dad, can you talk some sense into him?"

Before John could speak, Jeff spoke up. "Honey, you know spending money on you isn't the issue. I'd be glad to take you somewhere else or to buy you something nice. "

"Why don't you want to take her to Chicago?" asked Anna. "Her idea sounds like a lot of fun to me!"

"Well, I'm quite concerned about the rising rate of crime in the big cities. I'm even concerned about her going shopping in Peoria by herself."

Abby spoke up, "I have heard crime is really bad in some areas."

"I've read that too," said John. "I wonder what's causing that. I figured with lots of jobs out there, crime would go down."

Anna turned toward Tommy, "I bet you have some thoughts on that."

"I think there are a couple of possible reasons," answered Tommy. "First of all, unemployment figures only account for people that are looking for work. There are an awful lot of people who are quite contented to just get a check from one of our many social programs."

"Ain't that the truth." Jeff chimed in.

Tommy continued, "And they don't count as unemployed even though they aren't working. With inflation as high as it is, they're probably finding it hard to buy food and basic necessities. Because of that, they turn to crime to feed their families."

"That makes a lot of sense now," said Greg. "Just last week at church we took up a special offering for some of the older people in the church that were dependent on social security and retirement funds. As I recall, they were having a hard time making ends meet this year."

"I can certainly understand how tough they must have it," responded Abby. "With your new job and my job going well, we're making more than we ever have, but we don't ever seem to have any extra money. Everything's so expensive anymore."

"I'll second that," said Anna. "I'm afraid to go to the store anymore. It seems like stuff is higher in price every time I go there."

John turned toward Tommy, "You said there were a couple of reasons for crime to go up. What's the other one?"

"Even those that are working full time are like Greg and Abby." Tommy said, "They find out that prices are rising faster than their pay and even though they're working, they can't get enough money to meet their needs. I'm afraid that in the near future, we could all be in a really tough position. I think things could get a lot worse.

Chapter 9

The next morning Tommy came down to breakfast wearing an old t-shirt and faded jeans.

"Mornin', Tommy," said Anna

"Mornin', Mom. Mornin', Dad."

Anna dished up the fried potatoes. "Hungry, Son?"

"Yeah, I'm starved."

John grabbed the orange juice out of the fridge and brought it to the table. "Ready to head back to school soon?"

"I been thinking about that."

"Yeah, what about?"

"With everything going so crazy, I think maybe I should just stay here for now."

"You're welcome to stay all you want."

"Thanks, Dad."

John finished chewing a bite of scrambled eggs. "Would be nice to have your help with the harvest."

Anna handed Tommy another piece of toast. "I'm glad you're staying. Now's a good time to keep our family close."

"I been thinking too," John said.

"Bout what?" Anna responded.

"We've been under a lot of stress lately. Maybe we should all get away for a coupla days before harvest."

Anna took her last bite, "Sounds good to me."

"I'd like that, Dad, but I don't want to be a third wheel."

"No, Son, you and I could go hiking or something."

Anna started clearing the table, "We'd love to have you with us."

John picked up his plate and glass, "Next week, I'll go to the bank and get some money out."

Anna turned in front of the sink, "How bout using that emergency fund we have tucked away upstairs?"

"Nah, I wanna save that for a real emergency."

On September 3rd, John went to the bank. When he got to the teller's window. He filled out a withdrawal slip. "I'd like to withdraw $1,500, please."

The clerk looked a little embarrassed.

"I'm sorry, sir," she said. "But I'm afraid that we're only allowed to let people withdraw $800 a week."

"Since when? It's my money, isn't it? I have a lot more than that in this account."

"Well, sir, we have a new rule just this week that we need to limit the amount of money customers can withdraw at any one time. All the banks are doing this. Some of the big banks are drastically limiting the amount of money their customers can use. I'm sorry, but there's nothing I can do about it."

"Have you seen the prices of things lately? What can I do with only $800 a week?" John took a deep breath. "Well…at least we can use our debit cards for the rest of what we need."

The teller pushed the withdrawal slip back to John. "Well sir, I am afraid that the total between the debit card and cash out is limited to $1,200 a week."

"Why in the world is that?" By now his voice had raised a few octaves.

"The explanation we've been given is that people may use their debit cards to buy stuff and sell or return it to get cash and we can't let the banks be drained of cash."

"But, it's my money!"

"If you continue to get belligerent with me, I'll have to call security."

John's face reddened a shade. He turned and left the bank without saying any more.

When John walked in the door at home, he called, "Anna, Tommy!"

Anna looked up from the couch. Tommy sat across from her in a chair.

"What is it, Dad?"

"They won't let me get our own money out of the bank!"

Anna spoke, "Tommy and I were just talking about where we wanted to go for the weekend."

John responded, "It looks like we won't be able to go now."

"Maybe it's best we don't go anywhere right now anyway."

"You're probably right, Mom," said Tommy.

John apologized, "Sorry guys."

"It's alright Dad. I thought something like this might happen. Many banks have an incredibly small margin of cash on hand and when people start to spend their money, instead of putting it in the bank that could make some banks insolvent."

On Thursday evening, John and Anna were watching the evening news. The well-coiffed news anchor came on, "President Burke has issued an executive order that banks will limit withdrawals to $1,000 a week. Some banks have had to close in the last week, but the Federal Government is taking action to issue emergency funds to banks that are in need of funds. All banks will now stay open with these limits on withdrawals."

"John turned to Anna, "Well, at least our garden is doing well and we have that steer to butcher. We won't starve right away."

"Well, that is a comforting thought!"

"Things could be worse."

"We have enough to help Greg and Abby out too."

On September 14th, the family gathered for Sunday dinner. Tommy mentioned, "I just read that nearly 30% of the mortgages in the entire country haven't received a payment for this month yet. I'm afraid this will finish off many banks."

"Well," said Jeff, "that's no big surprise. What can they expect when people only get enough money to buy groceries? Luckily business loans can still transfer money between banks. We're still able to make our payments on the farm and equipment. You're really in the best position John, with most of your stuff paid for."

Abby spoke up. "You remember Hannah, one of my best friends from college? Her dad has a large orchard and produce farm in California. She mentioned on Facebook that her dad and a lot of the other farmers in California are talking about not taking dollars for their produce anymore. They're afraid the money won't be worth anything by the time they need to buy stuff for the next crop. Things are really getting scary out there."

"Wow!" said Anna. "If the farmers won't take money for their crops, that's going to make it bad for people in the inner city. They may not be able to buy any food at all."

"I have to go into Peoria to work," Greg mentioned. "I try to always stay on the busiest highways and stay away from any residential areas. They found one of my coworkers in a park last week. He was dead and his car had been stolen. He'd just cashed his check and the last time anybody saw him was at the grocery store. One of the theories is that somebody staked out the grocery store to find someone that had groceries they could steal."

"John, I'm really worried about what could be happening," said Anna. "I'm even concerned about going to the grocery store right here in town."

"It might be best if I do most of the shopping from now on," replied John. "It might not be safe to let a woman go to the store."

"I agree," said Jeff, "I won't let my mom or Sarah go into town anymore."

"I plan on doing any grocery shopping we have to do on my way home from work," Greg said.

"We're quite far from any big city, so it might not affect us," remarked Tommy. "But in the Weimar Republic in Germany, when they had hyperinflation in the 20s, people from the cities went to the farms and took the food when they couldn't buy it with money."

"If that's the case," responded Jeff, "we'd better keep our guns handy. You never know when we might need them."

"I don't know," John answered. "I think I'd find it awfully hard to shoot someone who's just trying to get food for their family."

"That would be hard," said Jeff. "But what if they decide to try to kill Anna or Tommy to steal more stuff from you?"

"Boy, that would be a tough position to be in," said John. "I just pray that God would help me in that situation to make the right decision."

After dinner, the adults gathered on the front porch and enjoyed the nice day. It was partly cloudy and about seventy degrees that day. It was one of those beautiful early fall days. The beans just had a little green left on them and the corn was starting to brown, signaling that harvest time was near. It smelled like Autumn and felt nice to enjoy the fresh country air.

The kids played in the front yard. "Wonder how many pleasant days like this we have left?" mused John quietly.

"Do you think you'll be starting on your beans soon John?" Jeff's question interrupted his thoughts.

"Yeah, I figure within the next couple of weeks I'll need to start. This week Tommy and I'll get the combine out and check it over."

"My dad's talking about the possibility of storing most of our crop this year. Even though beans are well over $20 a bushel now, he's afraid that if he sells now, the money won't be worth much by the time spring rolls around."

John nodded, "I can see that, we'll just have to wait and see what happens by then."

On Tuesday, John went to the store to get a few groceries they needed. He saw that a gallon of milk cost $17.

He whistled softly. "They sure value that," he muttered.

As he walked to the front of the store, an armed guard stood near the checkout. As he looked past him and saw another guard out in the parking lot.

He went past the store office and noticed that the owner, Sam Rhinehart, stood at the office window. Sam wore his usual white apron.

"Hey, what's with the armed guards, Sam?" asked John. "I didn't know our little town seemed that dangerous."

"Less than forty miles from here, in a store about this size, a gang from Chicago came in and cleaned out the entire store."

"Serious?"

"Yeah, they killed the owner and the clerks. I have 3-armed guards whenever we're opened and I have a shotgun here in the office. With as desperate as people are nowadays, I'm not taking any chances."

John chuckled, "Well with these prices, I suppose you can afford them."

Sam sounded serious as he answered. "I'm lucky to be able to keep this place stocked as well as I do. Stuff's hard to get at any price. We're just about to the point of not even posting prices. Half of the work we do is price changes. Bout everything in the store goes up nearly every week. Some times more than that."

As John drove out of town, he passed the gas station. "Almost $12 a gallon! Two weeks ago, it was only $7.50!" he exclaimed to himself.

That afternoon, he and Tommy worked on the combine to make sure it would be ready when the soybeans were.

"Tommy," began John, "What do you think is going to happen here."

"I don't know, Dad."

"Do you think I should store my crops like Jeff and his dad are? I'd rather get gold or silver for them, but I don't think any elevators are paying with that."

Tommy snorted, "Wouldn't that be nice?!"

John neatly arranged his wrenches in his toolbox. "The only thing they do is write a check that you can't cash. Then your only option is to deposit it in a bank account that you can't access."

Tommy started sweeping the shop. "That's a tough choice. I suppose you're best off storing it for now."

"Yeah, if things stabilize, I could always sell them then."

"Dad, if they don't stabilize, I'm afraid that the government will step in. If that happens, they may just seize everything."

John put his toolbox back in the cabinet, "Do you *really* think that could happen here?"

"Maybe."

"This is America, you know, the home of the free and the brave. How could the government just take our property?"

Tommy hung the broom back on the hook. "They've been seizing assets for years. Just look at what the IRS does. If you don't pay the money they demand from you, they'll come and take whatever you have till they get what they want from you."

After dinner, they watched the news. The attractive blonde announcer spoke, "About 30% of the produce farmers in California have decided not to sell for dollars. They are currently negotiating with China to buy their produce for either gold or Renminbi."

The screen switched to an interview with Senator Gomez from New York. "I think it's a shame that these farmers would consider turning their back on this country when times are a little tough, it's just not patriotic of them. I would consider them traitors. I don't believe the U.S. government will allow this kind of behavior for long. There soon will be action taken to keep the food that the public needs right here at home where it's needed."

In other parts of the news, there were announcements of several businesses that closed their doors for good.

Anna asked, "Whoever thought that watching the news would be this exciting?"

"Yeah," John responded, "It's the most exciting thing on TV now."

"We have to watch it every day, just to keep up with what is going on."

The following evening as they were watching the news, there were reports of riots happening in Chicago. "Authorities are warning everyone who doesn't live in the city to stay out. The governor has called up the National Guard to guard O'Hare Airport."

Thursday morning, John and Tommy got their guns out of storage. John had a 30/30 deer rifle and a .22 that he used for groundhogs. He also had an old shotgun that his dad had given him when he was a teenager.

"Tommy, we should make sure these work, just in case."

"Do you have much ammo, Dad?"

John stuck his head in the gun cabinet. "It looks like I have about a half a box of shotgun shells, no telling how old those are. We have 30 rounds for the 30/30 and 5 or 6 boxes for the 22."

"We should probably try them out to make sure they work."

"Yeah, you're right."

They walked to the back yard, "Hey, Anna," John hollered, "could you come out here?"

Anna stepped outside, "What is it, John?"

"I'd feel better if you took a few practice shots with us."

Anna picked up the 22. "You won't cry if I outshoot you, will you?"

"Let's see it, Annie Oakley!"

Chapter 10

Ken Johnson had been keeping an eye on what had been happening. Now homeland security officers picked him up every day by and returned him home the same way.

Two weeks ago, Alex had approached him in the hall, "Ken, you're too valuable to us to drive alone through the city. Crime is too bad. From now on, you will have an armed security escort wherever you go."

This morning, as soon as he arrived at the office, Amanda stopped him as he walked by her desk. "Alex wants to see you first thing today. I think it's serious."

He headed upstairs without even entering his own office. Grace gave him a nod but didn't even say 'Hello' as he entered the office. She simply motioned him towards Alex's door.

As he entered, Alex looked up. "Please close the door behind you." Ken quickly closed the door and took the chair in front of Alex's desk.

Alex cleared his throat. "It's finally going to begin. The President is going to declare martial law this Friday. He would like everything in position by then. We have most of our men in place and there are just a few more people we need to put in place. The man that had been in charge of the Midwest had a mistress that he shared too much information with. Unfortunately, they were both killed in a small plane crash in northern Wisconsin."

Ken's eyes widened, "That's unfortunate."

"That brings me to why you are here. I've assured those in charge that you're completely trustworthy. You've been chosen to take his place in Chicago. The only catch is that you will have to leave tomorrow."

Ken swallowed hard. He knew this day would come, he just didn't expect it to be so sudden. Nearly a full minute elapsed before he answered. "I can do that. I know that to make this the world that we all want, we're going to have to make some sacrifices."

"I know this is sudden. Do you have any questions for me?"

"I have kind of a strange request," replied Ken. "Can I have Amanda transferred to Chicago with me?"

"That's a surprising request," Alex raised his eyebrows. "You don't have a thing for her do you? I didn't think you were that type."

"No," said Ken, "I'm just used to having her there and she seems to know what I need before I tell her."

"Well," began Alex. "I suppose so, if she's willing to go. Your orders will be at your new office when you arrive."

"Thank you for your trust in me."

"No problem. As usual, three armed officers will accompany you to O'Hare and then other officers will meet you there. We have a plane reserved just for you."

"What will be our focus to start?"

"Initially, you will oversee the nationalization of farms and other businesses and the distribution of resources to citizens. You will also be given the full authority of the President to restore order and to see that all executive orders are carried out."

"With your permission sir, I would like to talk to Amanda and then take the rest of the day to pack and get ready to leave," said Ken.

Alex replied, "Of course. Don't worry about any of your workload here, it has already been reassigned."

When Ken got back to his office, he asked Amanda to meet with him privately. She sat across from his desk and prepared to take notes.

"Amanda, you know things are changing rapidly. In the next week, everything will change."

"I can see that coming, sir."

"I'm being transferred to Chicago to head up the Midwest division."

Amanda smiled, "That's a great promotion for you sir!"

"I would like for you to come with me and help me there."

Amanda stared at him for a moment. "I'm flattered. I assume that would mean a promotion for me too."

"Yes, it does. We don't know about pay yet, but with inflation going crazy, pay may not mean much now."

"Sir, you are on your way up. I think I would like to stick with you. When do we go?"

Ken cleared his throat and shifted slightly in his seat. "Tomorrow morning."

"Woah! That's soon. It only gives me this evening to get ready."

"Take the rest of the day off and a car will be there to pick you up at 7:00 tomorrow morning."

Amanda paused, "Ok, I'll see you in the morning."

The rest of the day, Ken spent packing and canceling utilities and other services. The next morning, the SUV showed up promptly at 7:00. The three guards helped load everything into the back and got him to the airport.

As the attendants were loading his luggage, another black SUV headed toward their gate. When it stopped, the door opened and out stepped Amanda. She wore a form-fitting suit with a short skirt. She looked professional but also stunning.

The attendants nearly fell over themselves trying to be the first to help with her luggage. It didn't take long for them to have all of the luggage loaded. Ken and Amanda got in the plane along with four armed guards.

They had more than enough room for Ken and Amanda to be quite comfortable in the main cabin.

Ken mentioned, "I could get used to traveling like this."

"Sure beats flying coach, doesn't it," responded Amanda.

"You know, I never even asked how much this job pays."

"Does it really matter?"

"You're right, probably doesn't."

Ken soon fell asleep. Amanda read a book for the remainder of the flight.

When they arrived at O'Hare, they were met at the plane by two more black SUVs. There were three guards in each vehicle. The guards on the plane stayed on the plane for the return trip.

Ken didn't talk much as the driver took the highway to his new office. As the driver dropped him off at the front of the building, the driver informed him, "Sir, your luggage will be delivered to your new apartment."

His new office was larger and much nicer than his old one. Amanda arrived right behind him.

"Well, what do you think, Amanda?"

Amanda looked around, "Sure is nicer than our old office."

Ken saw a thick envelope on his desk. He went into the new office and closed the door. He settled into his chair, opened the envelope, and started glancing through the contents.

Amanda knocked on the door. "Come in," he said.

"What would you like me to start on? I would like to get a good start on our work before tomorrow if possible."

"Let me fill you in on what's happening. The President plans on declaring martial law this Friday."

Amanda raised her eyebrows, "I'm not really surprised."

"We have a lot to get ready before then. I'm in charge of thousands of agents here in the Midwest."

"What do you want me to work on first?"

"First of all, I'll need a couple of lists. The NSA will be able to help you with these. I need a list of all of the potential trouble causers first. We need to know who's a threat and who's stockpiling weapons. The sooner we can nullify the threat from rebels, the smoother this transition will go."

Amanda paused a moment but retained her composure. "I'd better get started right away. Do you have a contact at the NSA to help me with these?"

"Yes, here is a name and a number for one of my contacts at the NSA."

"The next list we will need is all of the farmers and privately owned businesses. I know this is a lot of work, but I need these lists by Thursday."

"I'll do what it takes to see that you have them by Thursday afternoon."

"Oh, and one more thing Amanda."

"Yes?"

"Can you get me information on a John Bower? Alex asked me to keep an eye on him."

.

Chapter 11

Abdul and Ashley watched the news regularly. One evening after the news ended, Ashley turned to Abdul. "I'm worried about what's happening."

"I know, but this is Allah's will."

"You don't seem to care about me and the boys."

"I do, but I'm willing to die for Allah. Besides, we're safe enough."

"Well, I'm glad we have our neighborhood watch program to help keep crime down."

Abdul looked at Ashley, "We both still have our jobs, we won't starve,"

"I know, but I worry about this more than you do."

"I have always taken care of my family and I will continue to do so."

"That's true, but still…."

Abdul stood up, "No need to worry so much. I have to be at work early in the morning. Good night." He went to the bedroom and closed the door.

Ashley didn't work the next day. She went over to Linda's.

"Linda," said Ashley, as they were sitting at Linda's kitchen table. "How do you and Dave stay so calm during all that's happening? Abdul seems to take it in stride too, but he never gets worked up about anything."

"I can see that."

"There's a difference about the way you handle it though. You don't even seem to be unhappy. You and Dave act like there is nothing to worry about."

"Well," Linda began. "The difference is that Dave and I know who is really in control. No matter how bad things get, we trust God to take care of us."

"Abdul seems to trust Allah. That's what he calls God."

"But the God we trust is different."

Ashley looked thoughtful, "I can see that. You guys seem so full of...joy."

"Thank you. The worst thing that could happen is that we might die. Even then we know that we would be in heaven with Him. So you see, even though things are uncertain here, we trust the one who is solid as a rock."

"Boy, I wish I could be so sure about that. I used to believe that when I went to church. But that was before I met Abdul. He won't go to church with me. How can you be so sure about what you believe?"

Linda took Ashley's hand. "Ashley, I didn't always believe. At one time, I claimed to be an atheist. I watched my mom die when I was twelve. I had prayed for months that God would heal her."

"Wow! That must have been really tough."

"It sure was. When He didn't heal her, I got mad at Him and I guess I thought I could pay Him back for taking my mom by not believing in Him."

"Why was that?"

"In a warped way, I think I decided that if God wasn't what I thought He should be, then He didn't exist at all. Throughout my teenage years, I always felt kind of empty. I tried all kinds of things to fill that void. Since I refused to believe in God, I had very little morality. Basically, if it felt good, I would try it."

Ashley stared at her. "Well, what changed? The person you described to me sounds like the opposite of what you are now."

"When I was 19, I met Dave at college. He acted the opposite of all of the other guys I dated. He didn't party and he didn't try to hit on me like the other guys did."

"So what did you see in him?"

Linda stared at the ceiling for a moment. "Something about him that attracted me to him. For one thing, he treated me with respect. I couldn't get him to ask me out though."

"Why not?"

"I know now that he didn't believe in marrying a non-Christian and he didn't see any point in dating someone he had no future with."

Ashley turned sideways in her chair. "How did you guys get together then?"

"We had some classes together, so I asked him to help me with my philosophy homework. He's really smart and always got straight A's."

"I've always been jealous of those types."

Linda smiled at her. "It wasn't long before I discovered that he was a Christian. At first, I thought he must be stupid to believe in God. However, I soon discovered him to be one of the smartest and most levelheaded people I'd ever met."

"He seems that way to me, too,"

Linda continued, "I found out that he had come from a Christian family, and from the way he described them, it seemed like they could have been part of a Norman Rockwell painting.

"So what made you change?"

"We kept talking and he asked about my beliefs. I told him I didn't know what I believed anymore. He asked if I would believe whatever was true and to see if the evidence pointed to whether there really is a God or not."

Ashley got a puzzled look on her face. "How can you find evidence for whether or not there's a God? You can't see Him or hear Him. I don't see how anyone could know for sure that He's real."

"That's what I thought too, but Dave gave me a book by Josh McDowell that explained his search for the truth. Then Dave also explained why we couldn't have evolved, but had to have been created."

"But that's not what we're taught in school."

Linda nodded. "I know. Then, he explained why Jesus had to be real and why He had to be who He said He was. I already knew that Jesus had to exist because of all of the recorded history about Him."

"I never really thought about it much."

"Well, after I thought about what he had said for a week or so, I decided to become a Christian. Dave helped me with that."

Ashley thought for a moment, "So, how did you two get together then?"

"The very next week Dave asked me out!" she chuckled. "I think he had kind of fallen for me during all of our discussions. By the next fall, we were married."

"You know Linda, I wish I could have what you and Dave have. I used to have some of that, but I never had the calm confidence that you guys have."

Linda came over to Ashley's chair. "You can Ashley, all you have to do is ask Jesus to forgive you for your rebellion against God and to help you to live your life the way He intended for you to."

"I want to do that, can you help me?"

"I sure can. Will you pray after me?"

"Ok."

Linda bowed her head. "Dear Heavenly Father, I haven't lived like you want me to. I ask you to forgive me and to make me your child. Will you help me to live like you want me to from now on? Thank you for forgiving me and loving me so much. Amen."

When Linda opened her eyes, she could see tears in Ashley's eyes. "Did you pray that with me and mean it in your heart?" She asked.

"Yes, I did. What do I do now? Do I have to tell Abdul?"

"Well, to learn how to please God, we need to read the Bible and talk to Him regularly. Do you have a Bible? And yes, I think you should tell Abdul."

"I don't know what happened to my Bible." Ashley paused. "The thought of telling Abdul makes me super nervous. He won't like it at all."

Linda opened a drawer in the coffee table and pulled out a Bible. "Dave and I will be praying for you," she said as she handed the Bible to Ashley.

When Abdul got home, Ashley had supper fixed and the house tidied up.

After they put the boys to bed, they went down to the living room and sat on the couch together. He spoke first. "Do you have something going on with you? You haven't been yourself all night."

"I - I'm not sure how to say this. I'm afraid you will be mad at me."

"What could you have done that I would be mad at you for?"

Ashley shifted uncomfortably. "I became a Christian today!" she blurted out.

Abdul just sat there for several minutes. He stared straight at the wall. His features showed no emotion.

Finally, he spoke in a monotone voice. "If you want to stay and do your wifely duties here, you can. Whatever you choose to do, the boys will stay with me. I won't make you go to the Mosque, but the boys will go with me. We can talk, but we will not talk of this anymore and you will not try to convert me to be a Christian."

Ashley stared at him for a minute. Then he got up and went into the bedroom.

Ashley sat on the couch for a few minutes. Then she got on her knees in front of the couch. A tear ran down her face.

She took a deep breath, "God, I don't know much about praying, but here goes. Help me to be a good wife to Abdul. Help me to be a good example to my boys. Help me to be true to you, no matter what happens. Amen."

Chapter 12

Friday morning John went over to Jeff and Sarah's place. Thomas was out in the shop working with his dad. "Hey Jeff," John said as he entered the shop.

"Hi, Grandpa!" yelled Thomas.

"How's my little buddy? Are you helping your dad get his combine ready to go?"

"He said I might be able to help drive the combine this year! I'm big enough now."

"He's getting to be quite a helper," Jeff said. "What brings you over here? I figured you'd be getting your combine ready."

John held out his right hand, "Could you help me with something? I needed a press to finish this part that I'm making for my combine. I knew you had a good one. Would you mind helping me with it?"

"Sure, we could do that!" Jeff smiled impishly, "But before you leave, you better go up to the house and say hello to the girls. Samantha would be upset if she found out you were here and didn't say hi to her."

Nearly two hours passed before John finally left. The kids all gave him a hug before he got into his truck.

He took a different route on the way home.

When he got home he went straight into the house. "Anna!" he called. She came into the foyer.

"You were gone a long time. What took you so long? I bet you wanted to see the grandkids more than you needed Jeff's help," she teased.

He didn't respond to her teasing. Just then the back door opened and Tommy came in. "Hey Dad, all I need is the assembly that you took to Jeff's and I think the combine is ready to go. Do you have it with you?"

"Yeah I got it, but I saw something on the way back that I think you and your Mom need to hear about. On the way home from Jeff's place, I went past Clem's house. The front door looked like it had been kicked in and police tape covered it. I didn't see any of their vehicles there, but it looked kind of strange to me. I think we should try to call them and see if they are okay."

"Did you stop to see if anyone needed help?" Anna looked concerned.

"I stopped by the edge of the road. I didn't see anyone around, but I figured that the police had already been there because of the tape across the door."

"Why don't we call Pastor Rick?" Tommy suggested. "He's usually one of the first to know what's going on."

"Good idea Tommy," responded Anna. "I'll call him now."

She talked on the phone for close to ten minutes while John and Tommy tried to make out what was being said on the other end of the line.

After she hung up, John asked, "Did he know anything? He must have known something as long as you were on the phone."

"Yeah, he knew about it. He said he had gotten a few calls about it this morning. He said Bill had been over there yesterday and everything seemed fine. Then this morning, one of Clem's neighbors had stopped by there and a van had been there with a couple of Homeland Security guys. They had just shut the van doors and looked like they were leaving when the neighbor pulled in. Before he could get out of his truck, one of the officers came over and told him that he needed to leave and that this property is being monitored for criminal behavior by the Federal Government."

Tommy's face contorted, "That sounds really weird! Something sounds fishy about this whole thing."

"Did he say anything else?" asked John.

"He mentioned that he had heard of another family that disappeared too. He said they were friends of Clem's and they were big into collecting guns just like Clem. It sounds very suspicious to me. I think something is going on and I don't like it, John," Anna looked worried.

"I don't know what's happening either. I suppose for now we just have to keep doing what we normally do and see what's happening. Would you call Greg and Abby and make sure they're okay?"

The rest of the morning, John and Tommy got the combine ready, but their minds drifted from what they were doing. They were lost in thought. After lunch, Tommy went to check his emails. "Hey, Dad! Is something wrong with our internet connection? I can't seem to get online."

"It worked last night, I went on to check commodities prices before I went to bed."

"Well, I can't seem to get anything now. I checked all of the lines going to the computer and everything seems to be hooked up all right. Something really weird is going on. Maybe we should have Greg look at it. He's good with all this computer stuff." Tommy's voice reflected his frustration.

"Speaking of Greg, were you able to get a hold of them this morning, Anna?" John asked.

"I talked to Abby. She said they were fine. She hadn't heard of anyone disappearing around them. She said Greg went to work."

"I'm glad they're okay."

It rained the rest of the afternoon, so John worked on paperwork in the office while Tommy read a book. Anna did laundry and watched some TV.

After supper, they turned on the news as they did most evenings. Words scrolled across the screen that there would be a special report that evening. Then a reporter came on and said that they were going live for a special report from the President of the United States.

The screen switched to a view of a podium and a room filled with members of the House of Representatives. After a minute or so, a man walked to the podium and said, "Ladies and Gentlemen, the President of the United States of America -"

Then the President walked to the podium. He paused for a moment and then started to talk.

"My fellow Americans, I come to you this evening because this great country of ours is facing a crisis. Not since The American Civil War have we faced trials of such enormous proportions. This crisis affects every one of us, but just as we have in the past, if we work together, we can get through this. I am confident that we can come out a better and stronger nation!

"Now is not a time for panic, but to take the necessary steps to work through this and to cooperate together to become a better country to live in. There will be some sacrifices that we all have to make, but if we follow the ideas that have made this nation great, we'll all make it through this crisis.

"As your leader, my staff and I have come up with a blueprint that will help us through this crisis and keep everyone safe. You and your family's safety is of utmost importance. We ask that you cooperate fully so that we can do our job and keep you safe.

"Our first priority is to create a system so that you and your family will be able to get the food and other necessities to live and be healthy. We will be creating a new currency system with credits to ensure that everyone will be able to buy the food they need.

"In order to keep everyone safe, we will not tolerate lawbreakers that endanger everyone. We know there has been looting and other criminal activity. I put you on notice today that we will not tolerate this behavior. We must all share the resources that we have so that everyone will have what they need.

"There are also terrorist forces out there that would work to overthrow the United States government. They seek to resist every effort we make to keep you safe. To minimize their impact, we have had to close down the Internet temporarily. We do not do this to create an inconvenience for you but to keep you and your loved ones safe.

"Again, safety is our top priority. We will all have to experience some temporary inconveniences so that everyone can be safe.

"The Internet will be working on a part-time basis starting tonight after this address. There will be registration sites that we would strongly encourage you to log onto in the next couple of days. We will need some information from you so that we can make sure that you get adequate credits for your family.

"The phone lines will remain available until 9:00 at night. Because of the terrorist forces wishing to undermine our efforts to keep you safe, we'll need to limit phone access also. We know that you'll need to keep in touch with your families, so you can use the phones when available. We will be monitoring phone calls to try to weed out criminal forces that create havoc. However, if you're following the rules, you have nothing to fear.

"At this time, and for your safety, I'm declaring martial law across the nation. We're requesting that you stay at home and off of the streets until the authorities contact you with directions about how you can get food for your family. All law enforcement personnel will be working this entire weekend and in cooperation with the Federal Government to keep everyone safe.

"If, in the case of an emergency, you have to go out, be prepared to be stopped and questioned. Law enforcement personnel will assist you. We would prefer that you dial 911 in case of an actual emergency. The Nation's 911 System will be available even when the regular phone lines are turned off.

"Federal agents will be coming to your area in the next few days to assist you in getting your credits and being able to get necessities. If you live in the city, they will be going block-by-block and issuing instructions. If you live in the country, they will be coming to your home and assisting you.

"I cannot emphasize strongly enough, it's essential that you cooperate fully with the agents. If everyone cooperates, we can get through this transition smoothly and quickly. The agents do have the authority to use deadly force if need be to enforce the law. Please, for your safety and the safety of your family, cooperate fully with them.

"America is still the greatest country in the world. If we work together we can work through this crisis and come out stronger. There may be some temporary changes in the way we operate in this country, but it will work out well for everyone.

"Do not panic and do not acquire a doomsday attitude. Just as we came out better after the Civil War, we will come out better after this crisis. We will restore order to this great nation and provide safety and necessities for everyone.

"I'm confident that if we all work together, we can build a better and safer America. I believe we can rebuild America into a country where everyone is equal and no one will go without the basics of life. I believe we can all share in the bounties of this great land.

"Never let anyone tell you that America is defeated or on the way down. Instead, America is in a transition into a better and safer country for everyone. We will work together to create a better society for all.

"We have plenty of food and essentials for everyone. We will work tirelessly to make sure that everyone gets their fair share. I look forward to working with you in this great endeavor. The future for our nation and our children has never been filled with so many opportunities and so much promise.

"We will do whatever it takes to work for the good of all of the people in this great land. We will walk into the future together, working to make a nation and society that we can all be proud of.

"I want to assure you that we do have all of the resources in place to transition through this change smoothly and efficiently. There will be no need to worry about anyone stealing from you or about criminal elements harming your family.

"In closing, relax for the evening and wait for the proper authorities to come to you and assist you with this change.

"May we all look forward to these changes instead of viewing them as negative. I wish you all a good night."

After the speech, reporters hounded him with questions, but the President declined to answer most of them. John turned the TV off after the speech ended.

———

They all remained silent for a few seconds after the screen went blank. Then John turned to his son and said, "Tommy, this is what you expected, isn't it. You figured this would happen, didn't you?"

Tommy hesitated for a second. Then he spoke. "Yeah Dad, I did figure that this might happen. Unfortunately, they have no other options at this point. They have to restore order and this is about the only way they can do it." Tommy looked lost in thought, and then said "Um…" He seemed to change his mind and didn't say anything else for a minute.

Anna spoke up, "Tommy were you going to say something else? You look like you want to say something, but are afraid to say it."

Tommy looked at her for a moment. "I don't know for sure what will happen, but I know what I suspect will happen."

"What is it, Son?" John asked. "We're family here, go ahead and say what you think."

"Dad, I hate to say this, but I'm afraid that they will probably take the farm."

Chapter 13

Around one o'clock on Saturday afternoon, two black SUVs pulled into the driveway. Both of them had 'Homeland Security Police' emblems on the doors. John and Tommy had just gone back out to the barn after lunch. They were getting everything ready to start harvesting beans the next week. John stood in the doorway of the barn when he saw them pull in. John started toward them when they came to a stop.

He had hardly taken half a dozen steps when four men got out of the first SUV and three men and a woman got out of the second one. Except for one of the men in the first SUV, everyone carried an assault rifle. The last man had a pistol strapped to his side; he appeared to be in charge.

As soon as they got out of the vehicle, two of the men trained their rifles on John, the others aimed their rifles at the buildings. John instinctively raised his hands. Tommy came out of the barn at that time and another man trained his rifle on him. Tommy followed John's cue and raised his hands also.

The apparent leader called to him, "Please walk toward us slowly! Keep your hands where we can see them!"

When they were about twenty feet away from the driveway, the man said, "That's far enough, please stop now."

Then he addressed John, "Are you John Bower?"

John answered to the affirmative. "And who are you?" He asked in the direction of Tommy.

Tommy answered shakily, "I – I'm Tommy Bower. He's my dad."

Seemingly satisfied with the answer, he turned again to John. "Is there anyone else here?"

"Yes, my wife Anna is in the house."

"Please go get her and have her join us. Two of my men will go with you."

John opened the door of the house. He could hear the sweeper running as soon as he opened the door. "Anna!" he called. He heard no response so he called louder, "Anna!!"

The sweeper turned off. "Yeah John, what is it?"

"Could you come out here for a minute?"

As soon as she stepped out of the door, she saw the men with the rifles. She seemed a little stunned and just stood there for a minute. One of the men with a rifle said, "Please keep your hands where we can see them, ma'am."

John gave her a reassuring nod so she raised her hands in front of her.

The man in charge asked, "Is this everyone?" John nodded affirmatively.

One of the men got a metal detector wand out of the first vehicle. He asked everyone to hold their hands out to the side while he ran it all around their bodies. When he finished, two of the men and the woman came forward.

The two men gave John and Tommy a pat-down search while the woman searched Anna. Once they were satisfied that none of them were armed, the men with their rifles trained on them lowered the barrels of their weapons.

The leader said, "My name is Darrell and I will be in charge of this local area. I assume you saw the news about martial law being in effect?"

"Yes, we saw it last night," said John.

"The first question I need to ask you is do you have any firearms on the premises?"

"Yes, I have a shotgun and two rifles."

"Two of my men will accompany you while you show us where they are. Please do not pick them up yourself."

John led the men into the house and went to the gun cabinet where he kept the guns.

"Do you have the key for it?" One of the men asked.

"I don't normally keep it locked while we're home."

One of the men pulled out a bag and placed the three guns in it. They also took the ammunition in the case and placed it in a duffel bag. "Is this all of the ammunition you have for these?"

"Yes, that's all we have."

When they went back outside, Darrell spoke up again, "I am sorry about the way we came in, but we want everyone to be safe. Is that all of the firearms you have?"

John replied, "Yes, you got all that we have."

"I need to notify you that last night after martial law had been declared, the President made it unlawful to willfully conceal a firearm. If you have any firearms that you do not declare, the penalty is a mandatory 10-year prison sentence. We're going to search all of the grounds. So I need to ask you one more time. Do you have any other firearms on the premises or elsewhere?"

"No, that's all I have." John got a little more courage now. "Do you have a search warrant to conduct the search?"

"Martial law has been declared. I have the full authority of the President to do whatever is necessary to restore order and secure the area. We don't need a search warrant to search anywhere we want to."

While the other officers searched the house and the barns, Darrell talked with John, Anna, and Tommy.

"First of all, I need to inform you that according to executive order 13603 that was signed by President Burke on March 16, 2012, we will be expropriating this farm for the needs of the people. In other words, all of the farm ground in the country will be nationalized in order to provide food for everyone."

John didn't say anything. What could he say when someone had just told him that the family farm had been taken from him? His face reddened a shade, but his features didn't change.

Darrell continued, "I know this is a lot to digest in a short time. I know this isn't easy for you. Times like these are hard on all of us. I don't enjoy this part of my job, but I know that in order to make sure everyone gets the food they need, this is what has to be done. Here's a copy of the executive order if you need to see it."

John took the papers.

Darrell looked John in the eyes. "The next question I need to ask you is, do you want to stay on the farm and farm it as part of your assignment or do you want to be reassigned somewhere else?"

"What do you mean?!"

"Do you think you can continue to run the farm even though it will not be yours? If you need to give it some thought, I can give you until next week to think it through."

John stared at him for a few seconds, "I don't need a week. I want to stay here and farm it with my wife and son if I could. It's what I know how to do."

"I would like to see you be able to stay here. As long as the farm continues to produce and you do not resist the authorities, I see no reason why you couldn't stay on the farm. I am sure you know it better than anyone else." Darrell went back to his clipboard. He removed a card and handed it to John.

"This is your card to buy supplies for you and your family. Each member of your family will be issued 100 credits per person per week. Your assigned time to go to the supply store will be on Wednesday between one and four o'clock in the afternoon. This way there will not be a rush on things at the store and there won't be long lines. We don't need to have people standing in long lines wasting time."

John's face reddened another shade. "Are you telling me we don't have the freedom to go to the store when we want to?"

"I'm afraid so. Try to make sure that you get everything while you are there. If you forget something, you'll have to wait until the next week to get it."

John's eyes went to Tommy and Anna, then back to Darrell.

Darrell cleared his throat. "You won't have to buy stuff for the farm from your credits. We have requisition forms for any supplies you might need. Utilities will be supplied to your house at no cost to you. However, usage will be monitored to make sure that no one uses more than their fair share. Do you have any questions at this point?"

John glanced again at Anna and Tommy. Anna spoke up, "When will we be allowed to travel on the roads again and what do we do about gas?"

"Travel will be limited for some time to necessary travel only. That includes your weekly trip to the store and travel to get supplies for the farm. I do anticipate that before long you will be able to meet with your friends and family, but I am sure that permits will be required for travel to and from the meeting place. Gas will be rationed for the farm and the other vehicles."

Darrell handed John another packet. "In this packet are all of the requisition forms you will need. Also, there are productivity forms to be filled out weekly for the farm, and for the three of you. I would recommend that you take some time to familiarize yourself with them over the next few days. When you start your harvest, everything will be hauled to the grain elevator in town. Supplies will be distributed from there."

Darrell paused, and then asked, "Do you have any questions at this point?"

Tommy spoke up, "I know there've been a lot of looters going around the countryside looking for food and valuables. How can we protect ourselves since you took our guns?"

"Well, it may be hard to believe, but you'll actually be safer now. We're collecting all the guns so criminals won't have access to them. Besides, with travel so restricted, they won't be allowed to travel. All these things we're doing are for your safety and the safety of everyone."

At that time, one of the men who had ridden with Darrell came up to him. "We're done searching the buildings and premises. Everything appears to be clean. We found this roll of cash in an upstairs drawer. There's a total of just over $5,000 there."

"You can let them keep that. It isn't worth anything anyway."

The man handed the roll of bills to John. He took it and stuffed it in his pocket.

As the rest of the officers were coming back to the SUVs, Darrell turned back to John and said, "The phone will be turned off for the next three days. We can't take a chance that someone might call their neighbors and have them prepare an ambush for us. That would be futile anyway. I apologize for any inconvenience this may cause you. Also, as travel is still restricted, you won't be allowed to go to church this week. One of my officers or I will be around for the next few weeks to help you get everything set up to work smoothly under this new system."

Under his breath, John muttered, "And I thought this was a free country."

Darrell stared at him for a second then said firmly, "We have a national emergency here. We all have to work together."

John took a deep breath, "What do we do now?"

"For the next few days, continue to work the farm as you have been doing. In the evening, some TV programming will continue for your entertainment. You'll be able to access some government sites on the Internet if you have questions or want to get more information about how things will be run."

Darrell then turned to the other officers. "Okay, this location is secure! Let's move on to the next stop. We need to complete at least eight stops today!"

They all loaded up and headed back out on the road. John, Anna, and Tommy just stood there for a moment like deer staring into headlights.

Finally, Anna turned to John and said, "So what do we do now?"

"I don't know." His shoulders sagged.

John turned to Tommy, "Do you have any suggestions? You're the one who saw this coming."

"No, I don't know what to do. I s'pose we have to do what they say. At least we still have each other and I assume Greg and Sarah and their families are safe."

"You're right Tommy," Anna said. "We have to focus on what's really important. It's not our stuff, but the people in our lives." Turning to John, "Are you okay, Honey?"

"I'll be all right. It's just going to take some time to adjust to this mess."

"Wow, a lot can happen in little over an hour!"

"Yeah," John held out his hands with palms up. "Like your whole life can be turned upside down."

After dark, John went out to the shop. He took a shovel and a wooden box and went to the freezer in the shop. Luckily the officers hadn't looked clear in the bottom of the freezer. Moving a stack of steaks aside, he found the bags he had put there.

He pulled the gold and silver coins out of the freezer and put them in the wooden box he had. Then he took the box and the shovel around to the back of the barn. He dug a hole about two feet deep and buried the box. Then he packed the dirt back down and put some sod back on top. The rest of the dirt he put in a bucket and threw into the field.

When he went back into the house, he told both Tommy and Anna where he had buried the coins.

Chapter 14

The following Wednesday, they all loaded into the car to get groceries. When they were still a couple of miles from town, Anna remarked, "It's different that there aren't many other cars on the road."

Right after she said that, flashing lights came on behind them. John pulled over and the Homeland Security police officer came over to the door. Another officer stayed near the police car. He held an assault rifle.

When John rolled down his window, the officer said, "Sir, do you have your papers?"

John stared at him blankly, "What papers do you mean?"

"You need to have documentation giving you permission to travel. Where are you headed to?"

"We're going to the store to get groceries."

"Then I will need to see your authorization for your assigned time to acquire supplies."

John looked confused and then Anna spoke up. "Is this what you need?" as she handed the papers they had gotten from Darrell designating what time they were to get their necessities.

"Yes, thank you, ma'am." He looked over the papers.

"Your identification, please." They all handed him their driver's licenses.

He handed them all back to John. "It looks like everything is in order. From now on, if you travel, be sure to carry the proper papers at all times and your identification with you. You will soon be issued national identification cards. You'll need to have those with you at all times."

They drove the rest of the way to the store without incident. They arrived at Rhinehart's grocery. Everything looked about the same on the outside. There were a few other cars in the parking lot.

As they went inside, they saw an armed Homeland Security officer near the door. As they went through the store they noticed that all of the items had been priced in credits instead of dollars. There were a lot of bare spots on the shelves and there weren't a lot of choices in many items.

As they looked at the items available, John remarked, "Things are a bit pricey."

"Yeah", echoed Anna. "100 credits won't go very far." There were two packages of steaks left and they were nearly 20 credits per pound. Tommy picked up one package, "20 credits per pound! We won't be eating much of this."

Anna stopped beside him, "The rest of the meat isn't a whole lot cheaper either. Looks like we won't have meat at every meal."

When they got to the checkout, Sam was running it. He had a sour expression on his face.

John gave him half a smile, "Hello, Sam, how are you?"

"About the same as everybody else that's just had everything stolen from them," Sam said quietly. He glanced at the guard at the door. "I'm working here so that I don't get reassigned somewhere else where I don't know anyone. I assume you got the same choice as I did."

"Yeah, either stay and work the farm or get reassigned to who knows where."

"Yup, that's about it."

John stared out the window. "Hard to get used to."

"Yeah, after all these years."

"But, what can you do?"

The ride home was quiet. Tommy just looked out the window. Anna cleared her throat, "Well, I guess we'll have to adjust our eating habits a bit."

Tommy looked up, "Mealtimes might be a little different."

"It's going to be a bit of a challenge to keep everyone fed the way we've become accustomed to. I can supplement from the freezer for a while, but that'll only last for so long."

"If anyone can do it, you can, Mom."

After they got home, John and Tommy got the combine out and went to harvest beans. Tommy kept the trailer moved where John needed it, while John ran the combine. John smiled as he said to himself, "It feels good to be farming. At times it almost feels like things are normal again."

By 7:00 that evening, he stopped the combine. He motioned Tommy over with the truck. Tommy came over. "What's up, Dad? Is something wrong with the combine?"

"No, I just think it is time to quit for the night." John looked solemn.

"But Dad, I've seen you work till after midnight to get the crops harvested. It's still early. Why quit so early?"

"That's when I owned the farm. From now on, we quit by five o'clock. We'll work eight hours just like everybody else. If the weather stops us in our farming, well it's not our fault. That's just the way it is."

When they got to the house, Anna had just put supper into the car. "Is something wrong John? I was just about to bring you guys' supper."

"No, nothing's wrong. It's just time to quit for the night. We can eat here as a family. Maybe afterward, we can play a game or something. We might as well enjoy and appreciate each other. After all, that's about all we have left."

"Well, okay. I can get supper on the table in a short time."

As John swallowed a bite of mashed potatoes, he remarked, "Seems hard to believe it's not my combine or my ground."

Anna reached over and squeezed his hand. "It's hard to get used to."

"When I think of how hard my grandfather worked to develop this farm and all the years my dad worked here. And all the years I worked here." His eyes watered a little.

"We raised our family on this farm, John."

"Yeah, this farm has been my home all my life! I grew up here."

Anna looked at him gently. She said quietly, "Now, everything has changed."

John snorted, "In the last week, I've lost everything because of lousy decisions that someone I don't even know, in Washington, DC made!"

"It doesn't seem right at all."

John sighed, "No, it's not. But we gotta live with it."

"We still have each other."

The rest of the evening, they played Scrabble. Anna laughed when Tommy tried to use his name as a word.

"Why not, Mom? You gave it to me."

"It's not a word though."

John chuckled, "I forgot how fun it is to just be with you guys."

Anna smiled, "We used to just watch T.V. together."

"Now there's nothing on but public television and the news the government wants us to see."

Tommy chimed in, "Huh! That's not worth watching."

Around noon the next day, a Homeland Security SUV pulled into the drive again. This time only two guys got out. John came out of the house. The man headed toward the house.

"Are you John Bower?" he asked. The man appeared quite tall and slender. He walked with purpose and he gave the appearance of being quite strong.

"Yes, I'm John. May I ask your name?"

The man extended his hand. As John took it, he could tell the man had a strong grip. "I'm Andrew. I will be working with you. I report directly to Darrell and he has assigned me to this area. Could you and your wife talk with me a bit so I can fill you in with the latest developments?"

John's tone softened, "Sure, you can come inside and we can talk in the living room."

"That would be great," responded Andrew. "By the way, while I am here, my associate will be outfitting each of the vehicles with a GPS monitor. It will help to deter crime as we'll be able to track any illegal travel and respond promptly."

John's jaw stiffened but he kept silent.

Once inside the house, he called, "Anna, could you come into the living room? There's a guy here that wants to talk to us. Tommy, you might want to be here too."

"I'll be there in a minute. I just want to put lunch in the oven so it won't get cold."

When Anna and Tommy got into the living room, Andrew introduced himself, and Anna and Tommy both introduced themselves.

"I know you are ready to eat, so I'll try not to take too much of your time. First of all, I have national ID cards for all of you. Here they are. Look them over to make sure that everything is correct on them." He handed each one their ID cards complete with photos in the left-hand corner. They resembled driver's licenses.

"I'm sure you're anxious to talk to your son and daughter. After 1:00 PM today, the phone lines will be working again. You can call them then. I understand you've started harvesting the crops. They will need to be taken to the grain elevator in town. It's the nearest one to you and the grain will be processed there. Travel permits will be easier to obtain after this week. I understand you like to go to church. This will be allowed starting this Sunday."

Andrew paused and looked at each of them, "Any questions so far?"

John looked at Anna then toward Andrew, "I think we understand so far."

"Good, you will need to fill in the appropriate request forms to get your travel permits. Also, you can get a permit to meet with friends or family. You will normally be allowed up to one gathering a week unless suspicions arise about the meetings."

"Do you mean I have to get a permit to meet with my own family?" John's voice sounded louder now.

"I'm sorry Mr. Bower, but there are forces out there that would like to rebel against the U.S. government and undermine your safety. So for the safety of everyone, we need to approve all meetings. Here are the forms to fill out to get your permits. You can also go online to fill these out."

"Can't I even drive over to see my grandkids?"

"No, I'm sorry, but that's the law. That brings me to my last item. How's the credit system working for you? I know you've only had one opportunity to use it so far."

Anna looked Andrew in the eyes. "Well, you can't get much for 100 credits."

"We realize it may be a little tight for some people. We do have a way you can get extra credits. We cannot monitor everything, so if you report a lawbreaker to us, you can get extra credits. "

John whispered to Anna, "We need to be good little snitches."

Andrew appeared not to have heard him. "These extra credits will be every week once you earn them. People who break the law take from everyone and they threaten the entire system. So you're doing your country a great service by reporting them."

Tommy spoke up, "So if we rat out our neighbors, we get rewarded."

"I wouldn't use those terms." Andrew looked at all of them. "One other thing, your new identity cards serve as your credit cards and they can be scanned by law enforcement officers to let them know where you have permission to travel. It's probably still a good idea to carry your paperwork with you, but always have your identity cards with you. Is everything clear?"

The family nodded for lack of anything else to say. Andrew continued, "I'll let you get back to your dinner now. Have a good day."

After Andrew left, they ate dinner without saying anything for a few minutes.

"Well," began Anna, "At least this meeting was better than the last one we had."

"Yeah, but now we found out that we live in Stalin's dream world," said Tommy emphatically.

As he finished dinner, John stood up. "It's nearly one o'clock. We'd better call Greg and Sarah to see how they're doing."

It took six rings to get through to Greg's place. Abby answered the phone. Anna asked, "How are you guys doing?"

"We're doing okay. We get to keep living here. Greg got assigned to work here in town. He's actually working with the government computer systems. It seems like he's working for the wrong side, but at least he's working closer to us. And he gets to come home for lunch every day."

When they called Sarah, she answered the phone on the fourth ring. "Sorry it took so long for me to get the phone. I didn't know they were working. It took a moment to register that my phone was ringing."

Anna asked, "How are Jeff and the kids?"

"Well, the kids are fine. They went back to school today. Jeff is, of course, upset. That's nothing compared to Jeff's dad. He goes from being depressed to spitting mad. I sometimes worry about him. How's Dad doing with all of this?"

John yelled loud enough for Sarah to hear. "I'm okay, honey. At least you guys are fine. Family's really what's important and everybody's okay so far. Just tell Jeff and his dad not to fight them. "

"They know not to do that, but this is hard for them."

Anna's voice softened, "I know Honey, but we'll be able to see you all soon."

After she hung up, John looked at her, "I feel a lot better knowing they're okay."

"Yeah, me too."

The next day, John and Tommy took a load of grain to the elevator. As they were heading into town, they saw a banner over the highway. It read, "Be a Patriot, Report Lawbreakers, Earn Extra Credits!" and then it had a phone number you could call.

After getting back home, John mentioned, "I think I'll try out their requisition system and see how it works."

He went online to request gas for the farm. John had to sit idle for three days because they didn't have any gas for the combine. A full week later, the gas truck finally pulled in.

Two of the days while they were waiting for gas, they turned on the TV just to pass the time away. One commercial that kept airing displayed how people that didn't obey the law threatened and stole from the system. It concluded by telling people how they could help their country and their families by reporting lawbreakers.

The final statement in the commercial said, "Be a Patriot, Report Lawbreakers, Earn Extra Credits!"

Chapter 15

Ken sat at his large mahogany desk looking over the latest reports that Amanda had turned in to him. He turned to the section with the statistics on losses of officers during the nationalization of property.

Ken pressed his call button for Amanda to come into his office and she came in with her usual promptness.

"Amanda, I'm looking over these figures of our losses. I see we've only lost two officers during the changeover."

"That's correct."

"Is that the location in Indiana where the officer thought he knew the residents and didn't take a full team in according to our procedure?"

Amanda nodded, "Yes, it was. We had to send two teams in at night to secure it properly."

"I want to thank you for working with the NSA to identify problem locations. Due to your efforts, we were able to send SWAT teams in the night before martial law had been announced and minimize our losses."

"Thank you, sir. In a few areas in the cities, we were able to send in heavily armed military units to confiscate the weapons. This also kept our losses down."

Ken looked at the report for another minute. "Well, it all looks good to me."

The phone rang. Amanda instinctively answered it. "Ken Johnson's office, how may I help you?"

After a slight pause, "He's here right now, Mr. Cole."

She handed Ken the phone.

"Hello, Alex."

Amanda could overhear Alex's voice. "Ken, I looked over the changeover reports from the whole country. You had the smoothest changeover of all of them."

"Thank you, sir."

"You did a great job with your procedures."

"Those procedures were actually written by the man who held this position before me."

"You still did a great job of implementation."

Ken smiled. "Thank You."

"Not every area went so smooth. There were a couple of spots in Texas where the rebels were expecting us. We had to send in air support to secure those locations."

"I heard about that."

"I also wanted to congratulate you on the low percentage of total fatalities."

Ken looked at Amanda. "Thank you. We tried to make sure our teams were adequately armed to discourage resistance."

"I will make sure the President is aware of the great job you did."

"Thank you, Alex. I appreciate that."

Ken hung up the phone and turned back toward Amanda.

"Do we have the reports on how the relocations are going?"

"I'm compiling the relocation reports now. Initially, it appears that many people are cooperating and staying to work in the recently nationalized locations. That'll make our job much easier."

Ken nodded. "Good, and how is the extra credit program going? Have we gotten many people to use that program yet?"

"We're heavily promoting the extra credit program. We've had some people take advantage of it, but I expect usage of the program will accelerate as people get used to it."

"I agree with you. The current allocation of credits is designed to allow people to survive, but also to leave them a little bit hungry."

Amanda smiled at him, "There is one item I received in the mail today that I thought might be of interest to you. It's a letter from the President." She handed him the letter.

When he took it, Ken saw that it had the official seal of the President. "Is there anything else, Amanda?"

"No, that's all for now. I'll go compile the monthly reports for you from all of the regional directors."

"Thank you, Amanda, you do a great job. If there's anything you want for yourself, just let me know. I can get you almost anything you want," Ken said, smiling.

After she had left the office, he opened the letter. It had been addressed directly to him. It began:

Ken Johnson,

I want to personally congratulate you on the great job that you have done during this transitional phase. I know that these are difficult times for everyone, but I am confident that we can remake this nation into a shining city on a hill. With people like you helping to manage the great resources of this country, we can rise from this and become a unified nation that is good for everyone.

I want you and all of the other National Directors to know that I give you my full authority to act as you see best. I know that you will make decisions that are good for this country and for the U.S. Government.

I congratulate you on your superb handling of all of those who would rebel against the government. We cannot allow individual rebellion at a critical time like this.

I will be coming to the Midwest to inspect some government property that shows great potential. It could supply us with oil and help us to become energy independent. With the new changes in government, I believe we can get it to produce in record time. When I come there, I would be glad to meet with you and congratulate you in person.

Sincerely,

President Anthony Burke

The President himself signed it. Ken leaned back in his leather chair and looked out the window. He smiled to himself.

At lunchtime, he and Amanda went to a five-star restaurant near the office. As they walked in, Ken could feel the stares of the other bureaucrats.

He thought to himself, "I wonder if they are envious of my position or that I'm with Amanda. Whichever it is, I sure enjoy the envious stares. At times I almost feel like a king."

At lunch, Amanda brought something up. "Ken, you said you could get me what I wanted. The apartment that I live in is nice, but I'd like to have a nice house like you do. I'd sure like to have a maid to keep it up too."

Ken thought for a moment and then replied. "This weekend, you can drive around the city and pick out some places you'd like. Give me a couple of options and I'll see what I can do about relocating the current inhabitants."

"Thank you, Ken."

"No problem. I appreciate all your help."

She hesitated for a moment. "I assume I won't be questioned by police when I drive around?"

"As long as you have your official government plates, you'll be fine."

She smiled at him. "I'm really glad I chose to stick with you, Ken."

"Me too."

After lunch, Ken went to meet with some of his Regional Directors to present his plan for food distribution.

At the meeting, he outlined how the food from the farms would be processed and distributed to the stores or distribution centers. "At no time are the stores to appear full and completely stocked or people will think we're keeping food from them by rationing. However, we want to have enough available for people to think they still had a few choices."

He looked around the room, "From our research, we found that you don't want people to get too hungry. If they're starving, they might rebel and take abnormal risks. If people are just a little hungry, it will encourage them to participate in the extra credit programs."

He paused for a few seconds and then continued, "We have more programs to introduce, but we want to do them gradually. People will adapt to anything over time, as long as we don't rush things too much."

At the end of his presentation, there were questions to be answered. Juan, one of his directors, had a question. "Ken, on your extra credit program, we have a few people that are willing to use it extensively. The problem is that they get to the point where no one they are around will confide in them and I've had two of my best informers disappear. I suspect foul play. What should we do about this problem?"

"We've looked at this problem and decided that the best solution is to relocate people like this. I think this will solve both problems at once. They'll develop new acquaintances to keep an eye on and they'll be removed from a hazardous situation."

"That sounds like a great idea."

"Any other questions?" Ken looked around the room and called on another director who raised her hand. "Yes, Annette?"

"If people want to know how long martial law will continue, what do we tell them?"

"Tell them it will be lifted when we are certain everyone is safe and provided for."

After the meeting, it was late enough that Ken had a driver take him home. Ken lived in a palatial mansion on his own private 10-acre wooded lot.

An older couple that had owned several manufacturing plants in the city had occupied the house. After the changeover, Ken had admired the house and at Alex's urging, decided to have the couple moved to a retirement center.

"It's for their good as now they're completely taken care of. They're actually much safer now," he told himself.

As his driver pulled up under the portico, the car stopped and the driver opened Ken's door. Ken walked up to the massive doors that led to the foyer of the house. His butler opened the door to allow him to enter. As he stepped inside, the butler said, "Welcome home, sir." His tone sounded rather empty and lacked emotion.

Ken went in and sat down in the spacious living room. He looked around at the lavish decor.

He thought to himself, "Ken, you've come a long way and done a lot for your country. Hopefully, people will come to accept this new system and not try to rebel against it."

Chapter 16

At eight o'clock on Monday morning, John climbed into the combine. He stopped at noon and motioned Tommy over to him. "Tommy, it's time to break for lunch."

He and Tommy climbed into the 5-year-old black pick-up truck. "I'll say one thing about this new system, Dad, it sure does simplify things since we haul everything to the elevator."

"You're right Tommy. We don't have to figure out what to store in our bins."

"Our bins? I hate to remind you, but they're not ours anymore."

John shook his head, "I know, it's just hard to get used to."

"If the weather holds, we should be done by mid to early November."

"That's about what I figured."

On November 5th, the familiar black SUV pulled into the driveway. John wore a light jacket and was walking to the shop when he heard the tires crunch on gravel. He approached the vehicle as Andrew got out. John asked coolly, "Hello Andrew, what brings you out here?"

"I saw by the reports you filed, that you're done harvesting."

"Yep, that's right."

"I assume everything went well. You had a good harvest according to what you took to the elevator. Is there anything you need to get ready for next year?"

"Well...I mean one of the tractor engines needs to be rebuilt. It's lost a lot of power."

"Do you know how to rebuild it?"

John hesitated. "Yeah, I can rebuild it if I can get the parts."

"Get me a list of parts on a requisition form and I will try to see that you get what you need."

John sighed, "I s'pose it'll give us something to do this winter."

"Anything else you need?"

"Well, I'll just need a few parts for the other equipment."

"List them on the forms."

John stared at him for a minute. "Also, it'd be nice to get more credits. It's hard to get used to the rations we have now."

"I can't promise anything, but you've done well. I'll see what I can do for you."

"I'd appreciate that."

Andrew cleared his throat, "There's one more matter that I want to talk to you about. We've evaluated your housing and your workload and we've decided to get you more help."

John shrugged his shoulders, "If you think I need it. Will they just show up every day, and will I be responsible for them?"

Andrew took a deep breath, "You currently have a four-bedroom house. We've determined that we can close off a couple of doorways and utilize the basement kitchen. We can easily make the house into a two-family house. You'll still get the family room, but they'll have the living room. We'll send a contractor out here next week to do the alterations."

John's jaw tightened and his cheeks flushed. He spoke in a measured tone. "Three weeks ago I requested permits for us to have our family gatherings on Sunday afternoon as we used to do. I've not gotten a response yet. I've seen Greg in church on Sunday, but I haven't seen Sarah and her family since the takeover. Now you say you can get a contractor here in a week to take part of my house from me?"

Andrew's tone softened, "I understand your frustration, but we have a lot to deal with in the changeover. I'll personally work to get your request fulfilled."

He looked at his phone briefly, "The new help will arrive next Friday. If it's at all possible, I'll try to get your permits before Thanksgiving."

The following Tuesday the contractor arrived. He came to the door and Anna met him. "Good morning ma'am, my name's George. I'm a contractor or at least I used to be. I'm assigned to this project to make your beautiful home into a duplex. I'm really sorry about that."

"Oh, it's not your fault. You might as well come in and get to it. Where do you want to start?" Anna opened the door.

"I'll start by putting an exterior door off of the living room. I'll need to put a wall between it and the foyer. And then I'll have to close off some doorways. It's all here in the prints I've been given."

George started into the house. As he came to the stairway leading to the basement, he paused for a moment, "I'm afraid the plans call for closing off this side of the basement stairs."

"I figured that."

"I'm sorry but, you'll no longer have access to the basement. I see you still have furniture there. I can help you move it to your side if you want me to."

"You don't need to, I can have my husband and son do it while you're working on the new door." Anna went out to the shop to get John.

She opened the door, "John, the contractor's here and we need to move our furniture from the part of the house that's being closed off."

"Okay, we'll come in and move it. Come on Tommy, let's get this over with."

They all headed to the house. As they got inside, George had cut the drywall away from the opening where the new door would go. When he saw John and Tommy, he stopped for a minute. "Hello sir, my name's George. I'll be here for a couple of days so I thought I should introduce myself."

"I'm John and this is my son Tommy." John held out his hand. "I assume you already met my wife Anna."

George shook his hand, "Yes, I did. I want you to know that I don't want to be here dividing up your house any more than you want me to be here." George looked John in the eyes. "I assume they took your farm just like they did my business."

"Yeah, they took just about everything from me. I just work here now."

"Yeah, me too. I used to have a good business with six guys working for me. Now I just work for my ration card so we don't starve."

"That's about where we're at." John smiled wryly, "we used to do whatever it took to get everything working. Now we just work our eight hours and stop. It just doesn't pay to work any harder."

George smiled, "That's my story, too."

"I understand perfectly."

George shook his head, "I don't know what's going to happen here, but I'm afraid we'll have some mighty lean times ahead of us in this country. Well, I better get back to work so my productivity reports look good." George went back to cutting drywall.

John and Tommy moved the family belongings out of the basement and from the other side of the house. They took a lot of it to one of the upstairs bedrooms.

George finished up the job Thursday afternoon. After he left, Anna turned to John, "It's going to take some getting used to, to live in a smaller house."

"Yeah, I hate it."

"Me too. At least George did good work."

"Yeah, in another life, I would've hired him to work here."

Friday morning, Andrew drove in followed by a bright yellow older Mustang. John had just opened the door to go into the house. "Well, Anna, we might as well go meet the new neighbors."

As they were coming out of the house, a scrawny, pale-skinned young man stepped out of the driver's side of the sports car. His pimple-covered face was framed by dirty blond hair.

He and Andrew came toward them. Andrew spoke first. "John and Anna, this is Jimmy. He'll be helping you."

Jimmy nervously stuck his hand out. "Like the man said, my name's Jimmy. That's my girl over there in the car. Hey, Andromeda! Come out and meet our new neighbors!"

A girl stepped out of the car. She looked pretty in a trashy sort of way. She wore a lot of makeup and her gaudy high heels had several rhinestones missing. The girl also wore a black leather jacket and a short miniskirt. Her bright blond hair stood up on her head and looked as though she stood in front of a high-powered fan to style it.

"I'm here Jimmy, when do we eat? You promised me something good when we got here. It looks like we're in the middle of nowhere." She chewed gum all the time she talked.

"Andromeda, come here and meet our new neighbors," repeated Jimmy. "This here is John and that's his wife Anna, and this is their boy Tommy. He's about your age."

She looked them up and down. "Tommy's kind'a cute. He looks a little uptight though. Hello, neighbors." There appeared to be little feeling in the greeting.

She walked toward the house. "Let's go see where we're going to be staying. This looks nice, even if it's a little old fashioned." She disappeared into the house.

Just then a moving truck pulled into the drive with another SUV following it. When it stopped, four men got out of the SUV and opened the truck. They promptly started unloading shabby but brightly colored furniture into the house.

Anna smiled, "Jimmy, I'm sure you won't have everything unpacked for a bit. Why don't you and Andromeda join us for lunch?"

"Thank you, Mrs. Bower. It'll be good to get something to eat for lunch."

"At least you'll get a good meal before you get settled."

"I'm sure Andromeda'll like that. She misses her family. When you get to know her, she really is a lot of fun."

The men got Jimmy and Andromeda unpacked and settled in just before eleven-thirty. Andrew pulled John aside and talked to him in a low voice. "You'll need to help him get started with farming. He grew up in Chicago and he's never lived or worked on a farm before."

John gave Andrew a long look. With a touch of sarcasm in his voice, he said, "I'll do my best."

During lunch, Jimmy rattled on and on about his car, his friends, and all of the things he used to do in Chicago. Andromeda talked only a little. She also didn't eat much. She complained about having to move out here with nothing around and nothing to do. John kept his mouth shut.

"Well, what'll I be doing around here?" Jimmy asked. "I don't imagine there's much to do this time of year."

"Oh, there is always stuff to do here," replied John. "Monday we can either work on the tractor or mow the fence rows. We need to mow those once more before winter."

"Oh, I could probably help with the tractor. I used to work on my car. I'm sure it can't be too different."

After dinner, Jimmy and Andromeda went back to their side of the house.

That evening as John and Anna got ready for bed they heard loud music coming from the other side of the house. Anna turned to John, "Should you say something to them about that music?"

"Oh, it'll probably stop soon."

About two o'clock in the morning, John got his clothes on and went and knocked on the new door George had put in. He knocked for a few minutes, and rather loudly, before Jimmy finally came to the door. "Hey John, what brings you here? Do you want to come inside?"

"No, it's two o'clock in the morning! We're trying to sleep! Can you turn your music down?"

"Oh, sorry man. We'll try to keep it quieter."

John went back to bed. The music subsided a bit and he finally got to sleep.

The next night, the scene repeated. This time Jimmy said that he didn't realize that they would go to bed so early on a Saturday night.

Both Saturday and Sunday, no sign could be seen of either Jimmy or Andromeda until well after noon.

After church on Sunday, about two o'clock in the afternoon, Jimmy stood outside grilling a couple of steaks.

John and Anna were taking an afternoon walk when they came back and saw the grill going. The smell of steaks grilling made John's mouth water. He remembered they had a few steaks left in the freezer.

John turned to Anna, "How does someone like Jimmy get enough credits to buy steaks? Even with the extra 10 credits a week that Andrew got for us, we still can't afford to get steaks."

"I don't know dear. Don't worry about it. We just need to save a few credits to get a turkey and stuff so we can have Thanksgiving. That's if Andrew comes through on those permits!"

When they went inside, Tommy yawned as he got up from a nap. The rest of the afternoon, they played games and enjoyed each other's company.

That night the music quieted down a little. However, about one o'clock in the morning, Jimmy and Andromeda yelling at each other awakened John. She yelled something about being out here in the middle of nowhere. John just pulled his pillow over his head until he went back to sleep.

Chapter 17

The next morning, John and Tommy were outside at 8:00 as usual. They worked on putting some of the equipment away for most of the morning. They also got the mower out and hooked it up to the tractor.

"Hey, Dad," Tommy said. "When are we going to start rebuilding the tractor?"

John looked toward the house. "I thought we might wait till Jimmy got out here. I'm curious to see what he can do."

After lunch, Tommy took the mower and started mowing the side ditches. About 1:30, Jimmy went out to the shop. His shirt looked wrinkled and his hair disheveled. He rubbed his eyes as he walked in.

John briefed him on the basics of how the tractor motor worked and what they would be doing to rebuild it. Jimmy yawned and stared at John's shirt pocket as John talked.

Once they got started on the tractor, John began the conversation, "So Jimmy, did you grow up in Chicago?"

"Yeah, I grew up there. My brothers and I kind'a raised ourselves. My mom always worked, so she had little time for us."

John looked at Jimmy. "What about your dad?"

"Oh, he disappeared when I turned three. I hardly knew him. I met him once when I was twelve, but he didn't show much interest in me and I wasn't much interested in him."

"Is Andromeda from your part of Chicago too?"

"No, she's from northern Kentucky. Her parents still live there. We go to see them sometimes. She likes to visit her family, but she doesn't like to be in the country."

"How did she end up in Chicago?"

Jimmy looked out the window, "Andromeda went to live in Chicago with her sister when she was only 16. She just liked the lights and the partying."

"How did you two get together then?"

"I know we look like an odd couple. I met her at a party my cousin gave. I knew I wanted to be with her from the first time I saw her."

"So, what happened?"

Jimmy grinned, "I pulled the spark plug wires off of her car and then offered her a ride home. It took a few more dates, but she finally got to be my girl. She goes out on me once in a while, but I pretend like I don't know about it."

For the next half hour, John worked on the tractor. Jimmy handed him a tool once in a while, but other than that, he made no attempt to help.

John broke the silence. "Well, what brings you guys here? No offense, but you seem a bit like you're a fish out of water."

"That's kind of a long story. I realized soon after the changeover, that it didn't pay to work hard. I never did like working anyway."

John raised his eyebrow, "Oh?"

"No, man, the way to get ahead now is to report people. I knew my cousin kept some guns hidden, so I reported him. They gave me an extra 40 credits a month for that. Then I had a friend that dealt drugs for credits. I liked the extra credits I got, so I reported him too. They gave me an extra 35 credits a month for that. I reported a couple of other people and now we get over twice the normal credits."

John turned toward Jimmy, "Really?"

Jimmy nodded, "I tell you man, I like this system. I don't need to work anymore."

"Then why are you here?"

"I think they moved me here for my safety."

"I understand why."

Jimmy stood up, "Hey, I'm not stupid, man. I know I can't keep a girl like Andromeda for long unless I have something for her. I get extra gas too. And I can get permits easily. We go to visit Andromeda's parents once or twice a month. She likes that."

John rose to his feet and looked Jimmy in the eyes, "So, you really think this system is a good one? You think things will go well with this new order of things?"

"It sure seems to work better for me. Before this, I was a nobody. I had a few part-time jobs, but things were tough for me. Look at me now. I get twice as many credits as most people. I live in a nice house and I got a pretty girl. I'm doin' good and I don't hafta work for it!"

John just stared at him for a minute. "So, what do you plan to do around here?"

"Oh, I don't know. I'll probably hang out with you guys and maybe help out some. I'd like to get to drive a tractor sometime. That'd be cool."

Just then Tommy came back in the shop. "Hey, how's it going in here? I finished all of the side ditches. Do you want me to unhook the mower and put it away?"

"Sure, then maybe you can help us with this tractor."

Tommy looked at Jimmy then responded, "Be there in a few minutes."

That night when John and Anna were getting ready for bed, John turned to her and said, "I don't get it, I just don't get it."

"What don't you get?"

"What do you see when you look at Tommy?"

"Uh, I see a tan, healthy handsome young man."

"Right, and he's fairly muscular and smart too."

Anna smiled and looked at John, "Yeah. And I like the way he's always ready to help around here."

"That's what I mean."

Anna put her arms around John's neck. "So, we did good. What don't you get about that?"

"Well, what do you see when you look at Jimmy."

Anna shook her head and laughed, "I see a skinny and kind of pale young man with zits."

"And he doesn't seem able or willing to do much around here."

Anna wrinkled her brow, "So, they're a bit different from each other."

John looked in her eyes, "So, how can any system think that Jimmy is worth twice as much as Tommy?"

Anna kissed John, "Not sure what you mean?"

John relayed the conversation he had with Jimmy to her. She pursed her lips, "So they placed him here to spy on us."

"That's the way I see it."

Over the next couple of weeks, John and Tommy finished the tractor while Jimmy watched and talked a lot.

True to his word, Andrew made sure that John got his permits for his family to get together at least twice a month. This happened the Monday before Thanksgiving.

Anna got on the phone as soon as she saw the permits and called both Sarah and Abby. They both agreed to be there on Thanksgiving morning.

Anna bought a turkey on Wednesday. It cost 50 credits, but it would sure help to make Thanksgiving feel more normal. Wednesday night, Jimmy and Andromeda left to go visit Andromeda's parents.

About ten till eleven, Greg and Abby drove in the driveway. A few minutes later Jeff and Sarah arrived. John, Anna, and Tommy were outside hugging everyone as they got out of their cars.

"S'posed to be a beautiful day, Dad," Greg said as he hugged John.

"Yep, 50 degrees and sunny!"

Anna paused her hugging, "It's so good to see you all."

John grinned, "Anybody wanna ride on the four-wheeler?"

Johnny smiled, "Yeah, Grampa!"

Thomas and Samantha yelled at the same time, "Me too!"

John went to get it out of the barn. He pulled it up to the house, "Let's see, whose turn is it first?"

He grabbed Johnny and set him on the seat. "Let's go!"

They spent about 45 minutes driving around the yard, then they headed for the house.

As soon as John walked into the house, the aroma tingled his senses. The smell of turkey, mashed potatoes, rolls, and vegetables made his mouth water.

"Boy, that smells good!"
Anna looked up at him, "Be ready in five minutes, big fella."

When everyone took a seat, all eyes turned to John to say the blessing.

"Let's pray," he began. "Lord, You know this has been a tough year for all of us. But, today we want to give You thanks for all the blessings You've given us. We thank You for our family most of all. We thank You that we can meet here together. We thank You for our food and we thank You that we're all healthy. Lord, we have a lot of things we could ask for, but we just want to thank You for your mercy and protection this year. We thank You for Your love and we thank You for a beautiful day today. Amen"

"Let's eat!" said Greg. "Abby, you do great and I don't mean to offend you, but it's been a long time since I've had Mom's cooking!"

Abby raised her eyebrows, "Oh, and just what are you trying to say?"

Everybody laughed. Sarah waved her fork in the air, "I know that Jeff's smart enough to keep his mouth shut! But I have to agree with Greg, it sure is good to eat Mom's cooking again. You don't know how lucky you are Dad!"

Jeff grinned at her, "You're a good cook yourself. I can tell you got your mom's talent for cooking."
"Oh, way to smear it on thick, Jeff!" remarked Greg. "Leave me out to dry by myself!"

Tommy chuckled, "Well, I don't have to worry about offending my wife! I can say that Mom's cooking sure beats the food at school though!"

As the teasing subsided, John asked, "Jeff, how are you guys doing through all of this?"

"About as well as to be expected, I guess. I try to look at it as positively as I can. At least we don't have to make payments anymore."

"That's one way of looking at it!"

Jeff's eyebrows furrowed, "My dad's taking it really rough though. We need to spend this evening with them."

"Is your dad going to be okay?"

"I don't know. He seems depressed. He said that he worked hard all of his life and wanted to leave the farm and other stuff for his kids and grandkids to have as his legacy. Now his lifetime dream is all gone."

John shook his head, "Yeah, that's tough."

"I try to keep the farm going so they will let us all still live there." Jeff turned toward Greg, "What about you Greg, how are you guys doing?"
"Well, I feel like I'm working for the enemy. The government assigned me to help with the computer system and to work with the surveillance center."

"Sounds like its right down your alley."

Greg stabbed a chunk of turkey, "Yeah, we keep tabs on everything. The work isn't bad, but I hate what we do if you know what I mean."

Abby smiled at Greg, "Greg's doing really well. He works hard to help us get credits. I've been assigned to the hospital where I used to work."

Anna looked at her, "That's good, isn't it?"

"It's not bad, but we have even more paperwork to do than we used to have. All the new rules we have to follow are ridiculous. If someone's too old, there are a lot of things that we aren't allowed to do for them."

Greg swallowed his turkey and nodded toward John, "How're you guys doing? How's it going with your new neighbors? I'm not sure why they assigned someone to help you with the farm."

"I don't think they're literally here to help with the farm." He related what Jimmy had told him about getting extra credits. "I think they want him to spy on us as much as anything."

Anna smirked, "They're both some piece of work. They are definitely not like anyone around here. It's almost like they came from Mars."

Sarah leaned back and shook her head, "I can't believe they came in and just made you give up part of your house. "

"It is what it is," said John. "It's not what we want, but we have to face reality and deal with what we have."

"I keep thinking about Jim Rush," mused Anna. "Do you think he saw this coming nearly two years ago? Do you think that's why he left? I wonder how he's doing."

Tommy pointed at the ceiling, "In retrospect, he may have done the smartest thing. I should have seen this coming too. The signs were there two years ago. I guess I just never put all of the pieces together like Jim did."

John reassured Tommy, "Don't beat yourself up, son. You saw a lot more than any of us."

"Yeah, but I didn't see this!"

"Hey, you were the most informed. We should have been paying attention too. I should have listened better when Jim talked to me. I still have his contact information, but I can't use it. We aren't allowed to communicate much now."

After dinner, the adults sat around in the family room and talked while the kids put on their jackets and went outside to play.

John looked around at his family and started the conversation, "A person could almost forget about the events of the past few months and pretend that things were the way they used to be."

Greg nodded, "Boy, it sure is good to have pumpkin pie again. I don't know where you guys got all of the credits to put on a spread like you did, Mom."

"Well, we had some stuff left in the freezer. We could supplement with that while we saved credits for this meal."

"Your freezer can't last forever," mentioned Sarah. "You will eventually deplete that and then we will have to all chip in when we come over."

John looked at her, "It's getting kind of low now. But we don't want you kids to have to help with the meal. We'll figure something out."

Anna smiled, "I'm so thankful to see my wonderful family again. I'm just so happy to be able to have family get-togethers again."

Everyone else echoed the same sentiment. Jeff and Sarah left around five. Greg and Abby stayed until almost eight. It was quiet after they all left and there was no sound coming from next door.

The rest of the weekend, the three of them played games and talked together. John said, "You know, I kind of dread seeing that flashy sports car come into the driveway again."

Chapter 18

On December 3rd, John finished rebuilding the tractor. The next day, John and Tommy did several repairs on the barns to keep busy and to pass the time.

Tommy mentioned, "You know, you would almost think you still owned the place, the way you take care of it."

"Well, son, I just don't have it in me to let it deteriorate, even if it isn't mine."

Jimmy followed them around in the afternoon, but at times he found something else he wanted to do.

One time Tommy brought it up. "Dad, you think we should report Jimmy for not doing more around here?"

"No, I think he's only here to keep an eye on us. They don't really care if he works or not."

The weather turned cold after Thanksgiving and they had their first snow on the fourth of December.

Jimmy's turn to go to the store came on Thursday. Tommy went out and shoveled snow off the walks and swept them clear. He came into the house looking disgusted.

"I'm tired of this, Mom! I just don't like it."

"We're all tired of this, Honey. But we have to make the best of it."

Tommy shook his head. "Not this, Mom. What I'm tired of is Andromeda."

"What do you mean? She hardly comes out of the house."

"Except when I'm out there. All the time I cleared the walks, she stared out the window at me like I'm a piece of meat or something. Then when I headed to the house, she opened the door and said 'Hi Tommy!'"

Anna looked confused. "What's wrong with saying 'Hi' to you?"

"It's the way she said it and she wore some kind of frilly negligee or something. I know how girls must feel when guys ogle them. I just feel so uncomfortable around her." He headed upstairs to his room.

When John came in, she relayed the conversation to him. John shrugged his shoulders. "I don't know what to do about it. He'll just have to try to stay away from her. Luckily, Jimmy's there most of the time. I don't think she'll try anything with him there."

The following Wednesday when Anna went to the store, there were a few toys available. She bought less meat and used some of their credits to buy a few toys for the kids for Christmas.

When she got home, the familiar black SUV sat in the drive again. As she opened the door to the house, she could hear Andrew talking to John.

"Mr. Bower, since cold weather has come and we need to make sure there are enough resources for everyone to have heat this winter, we're changing thermostats. We have new thermostats that are remote controlled. It may take a little getting used to, but the temperature will initially be set at sixty-two degrees."

"Sixty-two? In addition to starving us, you want to freeze us too?"

"Now, we realize that this probably isn't what you're used to, but we have to be fair to everyone and make sure that there will be enough fuel to get through the winter."

"We always had plenty of fuel before."

"We do have a few electric heaters and they're offered as an incentive to report lawbreakers. If you know of someone who's breaking the law, they're channeling resources away from people who support this country. It would be your patriotic duty to report them."

Anna walked in at that time. "What's this about changing our thermostats?"

John looked at her and shook his head. "They're here to put remote-controlled thermostats in our house so they can control how much heat we have. Initially, they're going to keep it at 62 degrees."

"Oh, great!" exclaimed Anna. "What's next, are you going to regulate our toilets too?"

Andrew cleared his throat. "There's no need to be hostile. These are tough times for everybody. We can get through this if we all cooperate."

Anna glared at him. "That's easy for you to say!"

Andrew hesitated then said, "There's one more thing. Our food resources must be managed carefully. Until now, we haven't said much about hoarding food. But starting the first of the year, it will be considered a crime to hoard food and keep it from being shared by all citizens. This includes more than a two week supply of food in the freezer or pantry. We all have to share resources to have enough for everyone."

John bit his lip; his face reddened a shade. It looked like Anna would burst a blood vessel.

Andrew and the technician left, Anna turned to John. "They've really gone too far now! This is ridiculous! I don't know how much of this I can take!"

"Shhh, we don't want Jimmy to hear us." In a lowered tone of voice, he remarked, "Are you telling me they didn't go too far when they stole our farm and everything we've worked for all of our life?"

"You're right, but it's really starting to get to me. What can we do? Is there any way we can get out?" Anna sounded like she was pleading. As John looked at her, his eyes moistened.

Tommy came in about an hour and a half later. After he took off his coat and sat down, he asked, "Why is it so cold in here? Are you guys suddenly trying to conserve energy?"

Anna explained what had happened. He didn't seem nearly as surprised as they were by it.

As Christmas neared, they made plans to try to make it as normal as possible. Anna dusted the house as John and Tommy set up an evergreen they cut from the back of the farm. Anna came to check on their progress. "It sure will be nice to have the family here without worrying about what Jimmy might overhear."

John smiled at her. "It'll be almost like before."

Two days before Christmas, they got nine inches of snow with heavy winds. It closed off nearly all of the roads including the main highways.

Sarah called and said that Jeff still planned on coming. She said Jeff could go by Greg's and make a path for them with the truck and snowplow.

Christmas morning dawned clear and cold. John and Tommy cleared out as much space for all of the vehicles as they could. As usual, no sign could be seen of Jimmy out that early. Anna thawed out meat from the freezer. They would have roast and steaks for this Christmas.

When they discussed it earlier, John mentioned, "We might as well clean out the freezer for Christmas. They won't let us keep the food after the first of the year."

Anna agreed, "At least we'll have a good Christmas dinner."

At eleven-thirty they saw Jeff's truck heading down their road. Greg's SUV followed. Progress was slow, with Jeff having to stop and back up frequently to get the snow pushed off of the road.

Once everyone got there, the men helped the kids and women inside. Greg mentioned, "I see they got your thermostat changed too."

Anna sighed, "Yeah, but I have plenty of blankets if anyone needs one. Besides, we have enough people for body heat to help."

"Did you know that with these new thermostats, we could tell if someone is using auxiliary heat? Not only can we control them, but also they feed back an amazing amount of information to us."

Anna rolled her eyes, "Oh, I'm sure they do!"

"That's not all. They're actually experimenting with some of them to even record conversations for us. There I go; I sound like I'm on their side."

"It only makes sense," said Tommy. "Why go to all of the trouble of giving someone extra credits, when you can catch people by planting a bug in their homes."

John stared at the thermostat, "I certainly hope this isn't one of those. We could be in big trouble if it is."

"I think I know where all of the new ones are." Greg volunteered, "I'm quite sure that none of us have one."

Anna stood on a chair, "Time to eat! Everybody have a seat and let's get started."

They all were obediently seated and John said grace for the meal. He thanked God that they could all get together for Christmas.

Samantha got to the table first, "Boy, it sure smells good. I love coming here for Christmas!"

As they were in the middle of lunch, suddenly they heard sounds from the other end of the house. "I don't know why we had to come out here in the middle of nowhere! I don't want to spend Christmas here alone with just you!" John recognized Andromeda's voice.

"Baby!" Jimmy responded in a much quieter voice. "There's nothing I can do! Our car will never make it to your parents' house!"

"People made it here! There are cars in the driveway! Go get a shovel and get us out of here!"

Everyone had quieted down and looked at each other when they heard this exchange going on. John could see through the window that Jimmy had gone outside and kicked a snowdrift. Then he walked over to his car and muttering under his breath, he kicked the car. John looked at all the food they had on the table.

He looked at Anna. She gave him a nod back. John knew that all of their life, they had never turned anyone away from their door or table.

John got up and put on his coat. He walked outside to where Jimmy stood by his car. He came up beside him.

"Kind'a ruins your plans for the holidays, doesn't it?" he said quietly. "I really am sorry you can't meet with family today."

"Thanks, it's not your fault. I don't know what to do with Andromeda. She just doesn't understand that we can't go anywhere today."

"I'll tell you what, Jimmy, why don't you guys come to our place and celebrate the holiday with our family? We have plenty of food to go around."

Jimmy's eyes widened. "Do you really mean it!? We don't want to impose on you."

"I wouldn't have invited you if I didn't mean it. Why don't you go in and get Andromeda and then come in for lunch."

Jimmy didn't take long to disappear inside. After a couple of minutes, he and Andromeda came out looking like they had just gotten out of bed and pulled on some clothes. John took them inside and got out two more chairs. He seated them at the end of the table.

"Everyone, this is Jimmy and Andromeda. They're our neighbors. They'll be spending Christmas with us since they obviously can't make it to their family. How about we all go around the table and introduce ourselves and our families."

After the introductions, things were a little quiet at first as everyone wasn't sure what was safe to talk about and what wasn't. Then Abby broke the silence. "Where are you guys from?"

Surprisingly, Andromeda spoke first. "I'm from northern Kentucky and Jimmy's from Chicago."

"So, how did you two get together, then?"

"I moved to Chicago to live with my sister. I met Jimmy at a party. We didn't hit it off at first, but when my car wouldn't start that night; Jimmy proved a real gentleman and took me home. He seemed quite polite and after a few more dates, we kind'a got together."

John was glad he didn't have food in his mouth when she talked about Jimmy being a gentleman and helping her. He remembered what Jimmy had told him about that night.

Sarah jumped into the conversation. "What brought you two here?"

Jimmy let Andromeda answer that too. "We got reassigned to this location. There wasn't any choosing about it by us."

The regular conversation resumed with everyone trying to include the newcomers in it. They seemed to be enjoying themselves. It surprised everyone how much food Jimmy could eat for being such a skinny guy.

After lunch, when everyone felt full, the kids began eyeing the gifts. The pile appeared smaller than usual, but no one said anything about it.

The kids started shaking the gifts, so John had everyone gather in the family room and got the festivities started. John explained how they only had gifts this year for the kids.

Johnny acted so excited about the toy truck that he got. Even little Jenny's eyes got really big when she saw the doll that she got. In his heart, John thanked God that they were able to get gifts for the children.

After the presents were done, they got games out and while the kids played with their new toys, the adults played games until late in the afternoon.

As the sun started setting, Jeff mentioned, "We better get going. I'd like to be home before dark." Everybody bundled up and went outside to see the vehicles off.

After the trucks left, Jimmy turned to John. "I don't know how to thank you for helping us to have one of the best Christmases ever! Could you wait here for just a minute?" Then he disappeared inside his doorway.

A minute later he handed something to John. "Merry Christmas!"

John looked at what he had been handed. It was a bonus card with 100 credits on it. "Jimmy, you didn't have to do this. We weren't expecting anything!"

"I know, but I wanted to. I really appreciate all you do for me. You're one of the best men I've ever known."

He turned toward Andromeda. "Come on, Babe, we better go home."

Andromeda unexpectedly ran up and gave Anna a hug. She held on for a moment and then said, "Thank you so much for all you did for me and for being so nice."

Then Jimmy and Andromeda went through their door. John and Anna and Tommy went inside and cleaned everything up.

John looked at Anna, "You know, I'm not sure what good we did by having them over, but I'm glad we did."

"Yeah, me too."

Chapter 19

The New Year came in cold and blustery. There wasn't a lot of work to be done at this time, so John and Tommy spent more time inside. John filled out requisition papers for seed and other needed supplies for the farm.

Then he worked on the efficiency reports. He shook his head, "Man, it feels like I have to account for every minute and every drop of gas used."

In the middle of January, Andrew came out to collect some reports and for a field visit. John asked him a question he had been thinking about.

"Andrew, it's soon time to be thinking about spring. I wondered how I get seeds for the garden under these new rules. Does the store carry them and I use some of my credits to buy them or do I requisition them like I do seed for the fields?"

"Well John, I hate to tell you this, but there won't be private gardens anymore. All food will be grown by farmers in fields and the ground you used to use for a garden will now be tilled for the field."

"What do you mean by that!?" John growled. "Do you mean that we can't even raise a garden for some fresh vegetables for ourselves?"

"Sorry. The government can't control the safety of the food if everyone grows their own. This way we can regulate and monitor the food to make sure that it's safe for everybody. "

John's face reddened and his voice got a little louder, "I think it should be up to me and my family what we eat, not some bureaucrat in Washington!"

"You wouldn't want to risk feeding your family food that's unsafe, would you?"

"We've been growing our own food all of my life! I think I know what I am doing."

Andrew raised his voice an octave. "That may be true, but we have to do what's best for everyone. To do that, we have to have rules that apply to all."

Then his tone softened a little. "It won't do you any good to get upset about it. You need to calm down and work with us on this. Remember, I'm doing everything I can to allow you to stay here and work the farm."

After Andrew left, John related to Anna and Tommy what they had discussed. He told them about not being able to have a garden this year.

Anna's eyes watered. "John, I can't take this anymore. We have to do something. We can't live like this!"

"Anna! What can we do? We're stuck in this and we have to follow their rules or we'll be relocated where they want us to be. Then, we may not be able to see the kids and grandkids."

Tommy spoke up. "If there were only some way we could get out. I'm sure other countries are in better shape than we are."

John shook his head. "I really wish I could have seen it coming like Jim Rush did."

John began to see a layer of depression sat in over their family. Anna wasn't her usual cheerful self. Tommy slept more than usual and acted like he just didn't look forward to most days.

The temperature felt frigid and the days were short. John looked at Anna one evening late in January. "You know, winters are usually tough, but we always had spring to look forward to."

"I know! Now it doesn't seem like there's any spring coming."

John motioned next door. "It seems to affect Jimmy and Andromeda too."

"Yeah, we don't see them out much now."

"We can sure hear 'em arguing though."

Anna chuckled. "At least we know they're still here."

When they got together with Greg and Sarah's families, their conversations turned to how bad things were. There seemed to be very little good news.

Early in February, they had a family get-together. John brought up the subject of not being able to have a garden that year.

"Greg, do you know what they're trying to accomplish by this? Are they trying to starve us?"

"I'm not sure what they want to do."

"Without food in the freezer and no garden, we're totally at their mercy for food. With the current ration system, we sure can't buy much food to live on."

Greg sighed. "They don't let us in on that. I do know that they're looking at all kinds of options to spy on people. I suspect that soon, everyone will have some type of listening device in their home."

Sarah held up her hands. "Why? What are they trying to accomplish by this? Who's it helping? Soon we'll have to be careful what we say at our own family get-togethers. I just don't know how this helps anyone!"

Everyone stayed silent for a few moments, and then Tommy spoke up, "I suspect that it's all about control. The people in control benefit by all of this."

Sarah looked at him, "Why can't they just leave us alone?"

"You can't control free people. Those in charge don't want to lose that power, so they restrict more and more freedoms to keep people under their control."

Jeff shook his head, "I'm tired of all of this. I'm worried about my dad. He's taking this hard. He's getting so depressed this winter. He must sleep ten hours a day. I just wish there were a way out of this."

Anna sighed, "We all do. I s'ppose the best we can do now is be glad we have our family and just take it one day at a time."

John reached over and squeezed Anna's hand. When she looked at him, he gave her a gentle smile.

They made it through February and by the middle of March, the weather started to get nice enough that they went outside and took a few walks. By the end of March, they had a couple of days that were sunny and the temperature rose close to 70.

As the first several days of April were quite nice, John began to look forward to getting in the field. He started to think that they might be able to plant early this spring. Then it rained April 7th and again on the 9th.

A few days later, John started to get the equipment ready to go in the fields, when they got a surprise thunderstorm. The next day dawned cloudy and damp. The rest of April alternated between rain and damp cloudy weather.

Andrew came out to check on the farming progress. "How soon do you think before you'll get the planting started?"

John shrugged his shoulders, "Beats me. It has to be dry enough to get in the fields. We can't plant in the mud."

"Well, the authorities want at least 50% of the crop planted by May 15th. My area is behind. At this point, we have only a little planted. We need to move fast to meet the goals."

"Tell the authorities to make it stop raining. I can't plant until it gets dry enough."

It seemed like God took it as a challenge from the authorities. The first week of May, it rained every day. John measured a total of seven inches that week. Everything appeared flooded.

That week, they had to take an alternate route to get to the store. All but the main highways were flooded wherever the road crossed a river or large creek. A lot of the fields looked like lakes.

When it finally quit raining, the sun came out and the weather felt quite nice for five days. Andrew came back out to the farm. "Do you think you can start planting yet?"

"No, there're a few dry spots, but it's still too wet."

Andrew shook his finger at him, "Look, I'm getting a lot of pressure to get the crops planted. On the west field, I saw a lot of dry ground, why don't you try to start there."

John raised his eyebrows. "It may look dry on the top, but it's still wet underneath. It just won't work yet."

"This isn't a request anymore. I need to meet a few other farmers in the area. I'll be back in a few hours. I want to see some corn planted when I get back."

"Fine! It's not my tractor anymore."

John made it nearly halfway down the field before the tractor got hung up. He had half a thought to stay there and spin the wheels until he had it hopelessly stuck just to prove his point, but he figured he would have to get it out.

He walked back to the shop and waited for Andrew. He and Tommy straightened up the shop for a couple of hours.

John saw Andrew pull in the drive. He went out to meet him. "There's your tractor Andrew, I told you it was too wet."

"Can't you get it unstuck? What do you farmers do when this happens?"

John snorted, "Usually we have enough sense not to go in the field until it dries out. The only thing left to do is to wait for it to dry some more."

"Make sure it doesn't take more than a couple of days." Andrew got into his SUV and rushed out of the driveway.

That night it rained some more. In fact, it rained regularly for two more weeks. It was late May before it quit raining. No one had anything planted except for a half a row here and there where they had been forced to try by Andrew.

Finally, they had a week of dry weather. On Jun 4th, Andrew came out the day John checked the fields to see what would be dry enough to start planting.

"Is it dry enough finally?" Andrew asked impatiently.

"I think we can do most of it."

Andrew put his hand on John's shoulder, "John, I'm asking you to try to plant it as fast as you can before it rains again. I know you don't have a lot of incentive, but would you work later to try to get everything planted?"

John hesitated for a minute while he thought about all they had taken from him. He thought about giving a smart retort, but he also knew that it would be critical to get seeds in the ground soon or there would be no crop. "We'll do our best."

John and Tommy worked long hours for the next four days. Jimmy even came out and ran a few errands back to the barn for them. He seemed to like riding the four-wheeler and didn't mind being the gopher with it.

After the long days and short nights they put in to get everything planted, John relaxed for a few days. He figured that no matter how much it rained, at least they had stuff planted. Within a week, the fields were looking green with promise.

By the middle of June, temperatures were regularly in the 90's. Most days were clear without any clouds. It got hot every day.

Later that month, yards were starting to turn brown. The crops that had started so quickly were starting to show a lot of stress. The growth slowed way down. Cracks were showing up in all of the fields.

Late in June, the family got together on a Sunday afternoon. Jimmy and Andromeda had gone to her parents' place.

They were sitting on the front porch after dinner and talking while the kids played under the shade tree in the front yard. Electricity usage had been restricted, so they were seldom able to run the air conditioning. John looked to his left, "Jeff, what do you think about the crops this year?"

"Ours are about like yours. If we don't get some rain in the next couple of weeks, I don't think there'll be a crop. I heard they got a little rain north of here."

"I don't know how widespread this is, but it could affect the food supply." John sounded a little worried. "What do you think could happen from this Tommy?"

"If there's a big crop shortage and no one can keep or grow their own food, I think the authorities will start rationing food. They may come up with excuses to cut rations."

John shook his head, "Wouldn't put it past 'em."

Tommy nodded. "I'm really afraid of what could happen this winter. Food shortages usually affect the following year more than when they first occur."

Anna let out a breath, "I thought we were already on small rations. If they would let us have a garden, we could have watered it and at least had something to eat."

Abby held out her hands. "If they cut rations much more, everyone will have even less to eat. This feels like a downhill spiral to me where things just keep getting worse all of the time."

That evening John and Anna were talking while lying in bed. Anna propped her head up on one arm, "Honey, we gotta do something. I just get a bad feeling about things. I suspect they could get even worse."

John's eyes watered a bit, "I don't know what to do. I agree with you, but the only thing we can do is to try to get out. If we got caught, we could lose everything."

"We might lose everything anyway. I don't know the answer to this either."

John thought about their conversation for a couple of days. He thought about his grandkids, he thought about the crops that year, he thought about what those in authority were capable of and he thought about Jim Rush.

On the Fourth of July, John was deep in thought about what Independence Day meant to this country – and what it used to mean to him and his family. He made a decision. He would have to wait until their next family get-together before he could talk to everyone about it.

Chapter 20

On July the fifth, the skies were clear. John woke up and realized that even though the covers were kicked to the bottom of the bed, he already felt hot. He got up and pulled on his work clothes.

He could smell oatmeal cooking in the kitchen. He went downstairs and quietly came up behind Anna. He gave her a hug and kissed her neck.

Anna gently leaned into him. "Hey, who's disturbing the cook?"

"It's the milkman."

"Mmm, he smells better than my husband!"

"Aw, thanks a lot!"

After breakfast, John got up from the table. "Hey, you guys want to come outside before it gets too hot?"

When they got about fifty yards from the house, John explained his decision to Anna and Tommy. "So, what do you think?"

Anna pursed her lips, "I don't know, John."

Tommy stared at the sky for a minute, "That's a scary idea."

John nodded, "I know, but do you see any other options?"

Anna shook her head, "I can't think of anything better. Can you Tommy?"

"No, in the back of my mind, I've kinda been thinking the same thing."

Anna touched John's shoulder. "It's scary, but it's probably our best chance."

Eight days later they had a family get-together again. Sarah took her last bite of potatoes, "Mom you haven't lost your touch in the kitchen! We finish everything with your cooking."

Anna smiled, "Thanks Sarah, I wish there were more, but extra credits are nearly impossible to get unless you turn someone in."

Sarah nodded, "Yeah, I know what you mean."

Jeff looked at John, "Do you expect your crops to fail completely, or do you think there's a chance for any of it?"

"It's hard to tell. There's a chance of rain Tuesday according to the government weather report. However, much of the crop's looking quite brown. It just never had enough moisture to put roots down."

"We're in about the same boat. I've heard that there were a few showers here and there in the state, but most of us haven't had any rain for almost a month now."

John shrugged, "I guess at least we don't have to mow the yards. There may not be much work to do at all if we don't have a crop this year."

Greg spoke up, "At work the other day, we had a visit from some bigwig from Chicago. I overheard him and my boss talking about the crops around here. They sounded worried about the situation."

Tommy held up his fork. "I can see why. We used to be able to buy food from other countries, but now, the dollar's gone and they sure can't issue credits to other countries for food."

John snorted. "You mean like they do to us?"

"Yeah. Their only option is to trade goods for food. With government-controlled business, productivity always goes down, so the only way to have anything to trade is to deplete our resources like oil or precious metals."

Abby held out her hands, "So basically, we're just going to get less and less of everything until we run out of stuff. Is that the way it is?"

"That is the way socialism usually goes. The only people that profit from it are a few people at the top of government. Everybody else just gets poorer and poorer."

After lunch, John stood up, "Hey Jeff, why don't you and Sarah come take a walk with me to my back forty acres. I'd like to show you the crops there. Greg and Abby, you should come too. Anna and Tommy can watch the kids."

Abby hesitated. She thought it felt quite hot outside and the porch seemed much cooler. She just about mentioned this when she looked at John. She knew him well enough to tell by the look on his face that he had a reason for them to go with him.

"Okay, we'll go along."

As they walked, the grass crunched under their feet. The sun beat down, but they felt a little breeze and the air felt relatively dry. It wasn't humid, even though the temperature stood in the upper nineties.

As they started down the grass lane, everyone looked expectantly at John. He began, "I didn't want to talk in the house because I'm not 100% sure that the house isn't bugged."

Jeff nodded, "I understand."

"I already talked to Anna and Tommy about this and they agree that what I'm going to discuss is the best course of action. I've thought a bit about this and I think we can do it."

Greg looked at him quizzically, "Do what, Dad?"

"I've come to the conclusion that the only chance our kids are going to have in life is for us to get out of the country and to go somewhere else."

Everyone stopped and stared at John.

John looked around at them, "I believe we can do this. It won't be easy; in fact, it may be one of the hardest things we've ever done. However, I think it's better to try this than to suffer slowly for the rest of our lives."

They walked in silence for a minute, and then Jeff spoke up, "I'll have to talk to my parents about this. I'm not saying that I haven't had the same thoughts myself, but it might mean that my parents would never see their grandkids again. That's a sobering thought."

Greg's brow furrowed, "Dad, have you thought all about this? You know we can't drive out. We can't buy gas. We also wouldn't be able to use our cards to buy food. As soon as we try to use them, they'll know where we are."

Sarah's eyes widened, "If we get caught, we might never be allowed to see each other again. They might even shoot us."

Abby stayed silent. She had a serious look on her face.

John nodded his head, "I've thought about most of these things. I know the risk we're taking. However, we aren't living now. If we get caught or killed, that's just something that we have to face then. I don't believe that God intended us to live this way. We'll have to trust Him to help us succeed."

Greg rubbed his chin, "When would you want to do this?"

"I think we should start within the next few weeks. We'll need to cross into Canada, so we'll want to get there before it gets too cold."

"How long do you think it'll take?"

"I figure it'll take over a month to get there. Also, if there are any crops north of here, there might be some corn we could eat and possibly other crops available."

Sarah looked at John, "Wow, that's soon. How are we going to meet and start without Jimmy reporting us?"

"He and Andromeda always go to her parents place on the same weekend that we get to meet as a family."

"Yeah, like they are now."

"We'd probably have to leave on a Sunday afternoon. I suggest in two weeks. We'd have to be careful not to pack too much stuff because we don't want to attract attention and we'll have to carry everything we take."

The rest of the walk, they discussed various hurdles to the plan and how they could overcome them.

As they approached the house again, Jeff told John, "I need to talk to my parents and contact you. Let's pretend like we're talking about whether or not Samantha can come to stay with you for a couple of weeks. I'll describe our choice about that, but you'll know it's actually about this plan."

John cautioned everyone as they got to the crispy yard, "Don't mention or talk about this around any buildings. We never know when something is bugged."

As they sat on the porch watching the kids play, everyone stared out at the yard. They made small talk about the crops and about the possibility of Samantha staying with John and Anna.

That evening after everyone had left, John, Anna, and Tommy took a little walk while John filled them in with how the conversation had gone. They decided to use as many of their credits as they could spare to buy nuts and ingredients to bake apple and banana bread for them to pack along.

Three days later, Jeff called. Anna answered the phone. "Hello, Anna. Sarah and I talked to my parents about Samantha coming to stay with you for a couple of weeks. They said they'll miss her, but they want the best for their grandkids."

"I can feel for them."

"We'll plan on bringing her over in a couple of weeks. We'll have everything packed for her."

"I'm glad to hear that. We look forward to seeing her. We'll have everything ready for her."

That evening Anna related the conversation to John.

The next week and a half, they made lists and collected essential items. Anna baked loaves of bread and prepared packages of trail mix.

Jimmy spent most of his time following John around when John wasn't in the house. Andromeda did little but watch TV and occasionally lay out in the sun. Tommy tried to keep his distance from her.

That Friday morning, Andrew pulled into the driveway around eleven. John stepped out of the house into the hot sun.

Andrew greeted him warmly, "Hello, John. The reason I've come out to see you is that I've just heard from Chicago that the authorities want to have an emergency meeting to try to figure out what can be done about the crop situation. We've considered irrigation, but all of the sources of water near here are at desperately low levels."

"Oh, I believe that!"

"Yes, well the reason I'm here is that they want some farmers at the meeting to help with advice about farming. I thought of you. I think you're as experienced as anyone and you're quite reasonable to deal with."

John looked surprised, "When is it?"

"The meeting's this weekend, so you would have to come with me soon. You'd be well-fed and put up in a nice hotel. You'll also get an extra 100 credits for helping."

John chuckled, "That's thoughtful of 'em."

"I could order you to come, but I don't like to do that. Instead, I'm giving you a choice." Andrew rubbed his chin, "I have a few other farmers in mind, but I wanted to give you the first chance. Just remember, if you impress them at the meeting, it could be favorable for you in the future."

John stood there for a moment. He thought about the most prudent response. "Andrew, it seems like a good opportunity, but next week is my grandson Thomas' birthday. It's his tenth birthday and we were going to celebrate it this weekend. I really don't want to miss it."

"Are you sure about this John? I'm sure he'd understand if you missed this one birthday. He'll have lots of others that you can be at."

"Andrew, do you have kids?"

"No, I don't. I'm not married."

John stared into his eyes, "Then I wouldn't expect you to understand. If and when you ever have kids and grandkids, then I think you'll understand. They're more important to you than your own future. I wouldn't miss a meaningful time with them for anything. I appreciate the offer, but I really want to spend this weekend with my family."

Andrew looked at him for a minute, and then seemed resigned to this outcome. "Okay, if that's your choice. I'll get someone else."

As the SUV headed out of the driveway, John stared at it until it drove out of sight.

The next day, John expected to see Jimmy's car headed south by noon. When he came out of the shop at three o'clock and saw the colorful sports car still sitting there, he became a little worried. As he walked toward the house, Jimmy came out of his door.

"Hey, Jimmy, aren't you guys going to see Andromeda's parents this weekend?"

"What?" Jimmy retorted, "Are you trying to get rid of me or something? What's going on that you don't want me around?"

John stayed silent for a moment. Did Jimmy find out something? He wasn't sure how he should respond.

Jimmy gave a little grin, "Hey, just kidding John. Andromeda's mom isn't feeling well today. I don't know if we're going this weekend or not."

John put his hand on Jimmy's shoulder, "We'll pray for her."

"Thanks, John. I appreciate that. You guys are the real thing."

John went inside and related the news to Anna. To make sure he could be true to his word, he and Anna prayed together for Andromeda's mom.

John went back to the barn where Tommy stood busily reorganizing all of the hand tools. John worked with Tommy for a while. At about four o'clock, Jimmy came running into the barn.

"John, it worked!"

"What do you mean? What worked?" John looked puzzled.

"Your prayer, man. Your prayer worked. We just got a call that Andromeda's mom is feeling better, so we're leaving to go to her parents' place now."

"That's great!"

"Thank you so much! When we get back, I want to talk to you about this prayer stuff. There might be something to that. Have a great weekend with your family!" Jimmy had a big smile on his face.

"Yeah, you too Jimmy!"

After he left, John thought about their discussion. He realized that might be the last time he would ever see Jimmy. It wasn't that he felt especially fond of Jimmy, but he had grown used to him. He wished he could have had that talk with him.

On Sunday morning, John, Anna, and Tommy went to church as usual. There sat a sharply dressed man with salt and pepper hair in the audience. He had been coming for about a month. He didn't talk much but he had a pad that he typed on at various intervals. John had never seen him around town before.

Another thing that John thought about was that no one knew or heard anything about what had happened to Clem. He agreed Clem seemed a little different, but he always enjoyed talking to him.

After church, Anna prepared lunch as usual. She fixed more than they usually had. Greg and Abby pulled in at 12:15. Jeff and Sarah came up the drive three minutes later.

During lunch, the conversation turned trivial with a few awkward moments of silence. After lunch, Anna started to clear up the table and get the dishes ready to wash, but John stopped her.

"Dear, don't worry about cleaning up right now. Why don't you come outside with us? Somebody else can do the dishes later."

John and Anna grabbed the pack they had ready and headed outside.

Chapter 21

When they got outside, Greg went to the vehicles. He put the monitors from the cars onto the tractors and grain truck.

John got a shovel and went to the back of the barn and dug up the silver and gold coins he had buried there. After that, he went to the shop and got a couple of tarps, some ropes, a machete, and a hatchet.

Jeff took the vehicles after Greg finished with them and pulled them up to the farm gas pumps. He filled each one as full as he could. Meanwhile, the women were busy putting food and snacks in the various packs. Tabitha and Thomas had been told about what would be happening, but the other three kids just thought they were going on an outing.

Once everyone got ready, John divided the silver and gold that he had among the various vehicles. Greg brought along a slingshot that he had when he was a kid. He could take out a sparrow from fifty feet away. He brought a bag of marbles to use as ammunition.

John also took a collapsible fishing pole with him. Every family took some warm clothes, a light blanket, matches, knives, and other items with them. They had small survival kits with water filtration devices and first aid kits.

Once they were ready to go, John gathered the family around him. "I've laid out a route with an old atlas that I have. We'll travel together some of the time, but when we're around civilization, we may need to split up. We have an old set of walkie-talkies to keep in touch with each other. I doubt those will be monitored as much as cell phones."

Greg nodded, "I agree."

"Before we go, I want to tell you that I love each of you. Would you bow your heads and pray with me? Dear Lord, we ask for Your protection over us. We ask that You make us invisible to government forces. We ask that You provide food for us. We ask that You keep us safe from injury and from animals. We ask that you grant us favor with anyone we might meet. In Jesus' name we pray, Amen." John looked up, "Well, let's load up and go - and may God be with us."

Each family got into their own cars and John, Anna and Tommy led the way. They stayed on the back roads where possible. John prayed that any law enforcement officers would rely solely on the GPS monitors to locate people that were traveling illegally.

As they headed north, John saw that there were only a few vehicles on the road.

He used main highways when he crossed rivers, but stayed on country roads most of the time.

He drove the speed limit. The other two cars stayed back as far as they could and still see the vehicle in front of them.

Everything went smoothly for the first hour and a half. Then John saw by the map that a river should be coming up. He went over to the nearest state highway and headed toward the bridge. In the distance, he could see the silhouette of a car coming toward them. As he neared the bridge, he realized that it was a Homeland Security police car. His heartbeat went up a little as he passed the officer. He kept his speed at 55 while he kept his eyes straight on the road ahead of him.

After they passed, he kept his eyes on his rearview mirror. Jeff passed the officer and then as Greg's car neared the officer, John saw the brake lights on the officer's car light up.

"Oh, no!" he thought, "We could get stopped and arrested before we get a good start!"

Greg kept going without slowing down. John took a left turn on the next county road. He thought about going back and running interference for Greg, but he knew the rest wouldn't go on without him if he got arrested. He saw Jeff turn on the road after him and a minute later Greg turned onto the road. Immediately after Greg turned, the police car went roaring past the turn, gaining speed as he went.

"Thank You, Lord," John muttered. He thought about how far this country had fallen when a man has to be afraid to see a police officer just because he was trying to save his family.

For the next forty-five minutes, John drove without incident along country roads. They saw a few people out in their yards, but for the most part, the countryside was deserted. As they got further north, there were a few spots of green, but it wasn't a full, lush green.

Most of the crops in the fields were sparse and heat stressed. Nothing grew as tall as John's waist. Even the tree leaves were curling a little. Most of the grass looked either brown or a weird shade of yellow.

John stopped to look at the old Atlas he'd brought along. He also had a map that showed wooded areas and cleared areas. He had a good idea where they were at by what rivers and main roads they'd crossed.

He kept the air conditioner going full out in their car. The afternoon sun beat down on them without a cloud in the sky.

"Anna, You don't s'ppose anyone will notice we're gone till at least evening, do you?"

"I don't see how."

"Good. I hope to be away from the vehicles by then."

"Good idea."

After studying the map for a few minutes, John headed to where he thought there would be a decent-sized forest. As he drove along, they were traveling down a stone road with a forested area on their right.

Tommy saw the small break in the woods first. "Dad, over there looks like a grassy lane or road."

John stopped abruptly. He turned onto the grassy lane. He headed down it. Jeff and Greg followed them. John suddenly realized that most of this trip, Anna and Tommy had said very little.

John drove slowly between the trees. "This looks like what we were hunting for."

Tommy nodded "Hopefully, it's an old road and not someone's lane."

As he drove through the grass and brush, the lane became harder to follow. Once they were about a quarter of a mile off the road, the path disappeared altogether. All around them were trees and brush.

John pulled off of the lane as far as the car would go. He stopped the car and got out. Jeff and Gregg pulled off into the brush as far as they could get their vehicles.

Everyone got out of the vehicles, John raised his hand, "Okay everybody, let's get everything out of the vehicles and get the packs divided up."

While they were doing that, he got the hatchet and machete out. He handed the machete to Greg, "Greg, can you and Jeff help me to get some branches to hide the cars as well as we can?"

While they cut branches, the women divided up the packs. Even Tabitha and Thomas were assigned a pack. They had brought a baby carrier along for Jenny to ride in. She was a little large for it, but she would be able to ride in it.

After they covered the cars, Greg, John, and Jeff put on their packs. Greg also took the first shift of carrying Jenny. John looked at the cars. "I think they're covered good enough."

Jeff nodded, "Yeah, you'd have to be really close to see them."

John had the compass, so he took the lead. It felt considerably cooler under the trees. Gnats were buzzing around as they started. Nothing about the terrain was even and there were lots of brush and weeds to walk through.

John looked back at Anna, "Boy, it's not like taking a walk along the road, is it?"

"It's a bit harder."

Occasionally, they walked on an animal trail, but those were a lot smaller than regular walk paths.

He stopped and turned around. "I want to put as much distance as we can between us and the cars today."

Tommy shifted his pack, "I agree. If they find the cars, we don't want to be anywhere near them."

After about a half of a mile, Samantha rubbed her legs, "Daddy, I don't like these weeds, they stick me. Can't we stop yet? When can we go home?"

Jeff touched her shoulder, "Honey, we aren't going home today. Remember, I told you that we were going camping for a while."

"How long!?"

"We're going to walk through the woods for this afternoon. Let's see who can spot the most animals. You can pretend that we're Indians and we have to sneak up on animals."

"But, my legs are tired. I wish you could carry me like Uncle Greg carries Jenny."

"I do too, sweetheart, but you're getting too big to carry for a long time. Maybe later, I can carry you for a little while."

Johnny came up beside her, "I don't need to be carried. My daddy said I could pretend to be Daniel Boone. Sam, we can pretend to be explorers looking for the ocean."

"I'm a girl!" Samantha retorted, "Girls aren't explorers."

"Daddy said there was an Indian girl that went with Clark and Lews," Johnny said cheerfully. "You could pretend like that girl is you!"

Samantha sighed, "I s'ppose, I'll try but I'm getting tired."

After about a mile, they came to a clearing. The sun dropped a little lower, so the heat wasn't quite as intense. There were more woods about a quarter of a mile ahead of them. Above them, an electric line suspended on poles stretched across the clearing.

They stopped at the edge of the clearing. John looked across the grass. "What do you guys think? Do you think it's safe to cross the clearing in daylight?"

Greg rubbed his chin, "We might have to risk it. I think we should go a few at a time though to attract less attention." Everyone agreed to that and John went first.

He bent down by Samantha and hoisted her to his shoulders. "Do you want to pretend that I'm your horse and you can ride me over to those other woods?"

Samantha giggled, "You're not a horse Grandpa, but you can be my riding cow!"

The rest of the group chuckled.

As John crossed the clearing, the grass crunched under his feet, but he could feel a softer layer underneath the crispy tops. John resisted the urge to cross as fast as possible. He looked at Anna, "If we're seen crossing here, we don't want to look like we're running from something."

After their group got across without incident, Jeff and Sarah came with the two older kids. After that, Greg and Abby crossed the clearing.

By now, shadows were getting long. Sarah looked at John, "Dad, how long before we stop for the night?"

Abby nodded, "I'm certainly not used to this."

Anna put her hand on John's arm, "We're all starting to feel this, honey."

John looked at everyone, "I know this is tough, but we need to put a little more distance between us and the vehicles. We can't take a chance on getting caught before we get a good start."

John took the lead. Everyone else followed.

As they got deeper into the forest, it got darker. John found it difficult to tell where they were going some of the time. Tommy followed right behind him at this point. "Hey, Dad, we probably shouldn't use the flashlights unless we absolutely have to."

John nodded, "I agree, we're too close to civilization."

Just when he began to think he might have to turn on the flashlight, John saw that it got lighter ahead of them.

As the path got less dim, John realized they had come to another clearing. He stopped near the edge and peered out. He saw a large field of stunted soybeans. As everyone got near the edge of the woods, they all stopped behind John.

"I think we'd better wait here till it gets a little darker."

Jeff stood beside John, "How long do you think we should wait?"

"We probably have a half an hour. We can rest and maybe eat a little."

"How long before we stop for the night?"

"I'd like to do at least a couple more miles before we stop to camp. It should go quicker if we can go across the fields, but we'll have to be quiet. Sound will travel easier out in the open."

They all trampled down some brush to get comfortable. There laid a fallen log to sit on. After nibbling on some of the snacks they had brought, John decided it seemed dark enough to move out. John used the light from his watch to check the compass and make sure they were headed in the right direction.

They crossed a fence and then another field. In the distance, the lights of a house were visible. They came to a road. John couldn't make out the road sign, but he figured that they were still in Illinois.

It was a stone road and they didn't see anyone on the road so they crossed it. Anna tripped when she got to the other side and stepped in the side ditch. John helped her up. "Are you okay, Honey?"

"I think so, it's just so dark out here that I have trouble seeing where I'm going."

John checked his compass again and they started across the next field. When they came to the second field row, it just had grass and a few trees to mark it. As they started across that field, John thought the crops looked odd. "Tomatoes!" he exclaimed. "This is a tomato field."

He wondered why they were so nice until he saw the silhouette of the irrigation line a little distance away.

"See if you can find any ripe ones to take. Also, eat some now if you want to."

John found a few ripe ones. Everyone else foraged for more.

After they ate a few tomatoes and got some to go, they continued across the field to the next road. On the other side of the road, stood a woods. "Do any of you see any sign of houses near here?"

Greg looked both ways. "I don't see anything, Dad."

Tommy came up to them, "Me neither."

John nodded, "This wooded area might be a good place to camp."

After stumbling through for about a hundred yards, they found a thicket of evergreens with about four feet of space under the lower branches.

They stopped and the men cut some of the branches as a cushion under their blankets. By the time they were done, little Johnny and Samantha were sitting down and already asleep. Everyone else fell asleep quickly.

Chapter 22

After the weekend, Jimmy and Andromeda got back to the farm about 9:00 Sunday evening. Everything looked quiet when they pulled in. Jimmy looked at the parking area. "I don't see John's car. That's odd."

Andromeda glanced around, "Me neither. Who knows?"

"Maybe he has it in the shop."

"That's possible. Seems awfully quiet around here."

Jimmy nodded. "Maybe, they went to bed early."

"Yeah, they do that."

He and Andromeda stayed up late as usual and then slept in.

The next day, he went outside just after noon. He felt a hot dry breeze blowing but nothing else appeared to be moving. No sign of anyone could be seen on the farm. Jimmy went to the shop and looked inside. The shop appeared empty and John's car could not be seen. Tommy's VW Beetle was parked under the tree like it had been when they left.

"This is weird!" thought Jimmy. "It's like everyone has just vanished."

Jimmy went back to the house. He opened the front door, "Andromeda!"

"What do ya want?" Andromeda yelled.

Jimmy went into the living room where she wats watching TV. "Something's wrong Andromeda! There's no one around anywhere! I don't see any sign of John or Tommy."

"That's strange. Where are they?"

Jimmy wrinkled his brow, "Hey, I remember hearing a TV preacher talking about something called the rapture. He said Christians would disappear in an instant."

"Do you think that's what happened?"

"I dunno. Wait a second. Their car's gone too! I don't think their cars would go with 'em."

"Do you think they were murdered? Have you checked the house to see if they're there?" Andromeda asked frantically.

"I hadn't thought of that. Maybe whoever did it stole their car!"

Andromeda's face paled, "We better call the authorities!"

"We oughta check their side of the house before we call someone."

Andromeda pointed at him, "You can go over there! I'm not going to find any dead bodies. That's too creepy for me!"

Jimmy went over to the main door of the house. He knocked several times. No one answered. He tried the doorknob. It opened easily. Jimmy went in slowly. "John!? Anna!? Tommy!?" He waited for a moment. Nothing but silence. He fought the rising fear in his stomach.

Jimmy went into the kitchen. Dirty dishes and a few leftovers were sitting on the kitchen table. Anna always seemed so neat and clean. Jimmy couldn't imagine her leaving things this way unless something beyond her control had happened to them.

He went over to the foot of the stairs. Maybe they were forced to go upstairs before they were murdered! He could feel the hair rising on the back of his neck as he made his way up the stairs.

He slowly opened each of the bedroom doors. Each bedroom appeared neat and clean with the beds made. Nothing seemed out of place. The bathroom seemed equally neat and clean.

The entire home except for the kitchen looked like they were gone for vacation and were expecting to return in a little while.

He went back over to his side of the house. Andromeda met him when he came into the house. "Well, what did you find?"

"I think they took off and left us! It looks like they skipped completely."

"Are you going to call it in?"

Jimmy swallowed hard "Yeah, I better do that. We might get in trouble if we don't and we might get more credits if we do."

He picked up his phone and dialed the reporting hotline. A lady answered the phone. "Thank you for being a patriot, may I have the nature of the violation you wish to report?"

"I think someone's taken off. They seem to have disappeared."

"Can I have the name and the address of the person you wish to report?"

"The name is John Bower." Then he gave her the address.

"Give me just a second to check on that." After a pause for a few minutes, "Do you think they left on foot? According to our system, his car is still at the farm."

"Oh, I've been in all of the buildings. I'm quite sure his car isn't here."

"We're showing his car right there." Another slight pause. "Wait a second, this is odd. I'm showing that his visitor's cars are still there also. They only had a permit to meet for yesterday. They should be gone by now. Are there extra cars there?"

"No. No, there aren't any extra cars here. Maybe they all took off together."

"I'll file this report. The authorities should be there soon. Try to answer all of their questions to the best of your ability and we'll see that you get your extra credits."

Jimmy went outside and sat on the front porch to wait on the expected entourage. Within 15 minutes two SUVs pulled into the driveway. Four men piled out of each vehicle. Andrew was one of them.

He approached the front porch. "Jimmy, thank you for calling this in. We'll be searching the entire premises to look for evidence. We'll also have to search your residence."

"Why do you have to search my home? I didn't do nothing wrong! I'm the one that reported this."

"Calm down Jimmy, we just need to cover all our bases. We have to clear you in this. Desertion is a very serious charge and we need to make sure you're completely innocent. Darrell will be here in about 45 minutes. By then we should have something to report to him."

Jimmy frowned but kept quiet. He went with Andrew to the front door of his side of the home. "Andromeda! They need to search our side of the house!"

Andromeda peeked around the corner. "Why do they have to come in here? We didn't take off!"

"Yeah, Babe, I know, but they have to. It would probably be better if you came out here while they search."

Andromeda did as he told her.

During the next 40 minutes, the men searched every drawer, and cabinet in the house and buildings. They weren't real neat about putting things back.

By the time Darrell arrived, the search was winding down. Andrew met Darrell and then invited Jimmy and Andromeda to sit with them on the front porch while they talked.

Darrell took a seat and turned toward Jimmy, "So, Jimmy, when did you first notice something wrong?"

"Well, last night when we got back from Andromeda's parents, I noticed that things seemed a little quieter than normal."

"Why didn't you call it in then? You've been good about reporting lawbreakers before."

Jimmy shifted in his chair. "I just thought that maybe they went to bed early. Sometimes they go to bed crazy early over there."

"I have trouble understanding how it is nearly 24 hours after it appears they left, that you called the authorities. Are you trying to help them?" Darrell's voice showed no emotion.

"Hey, I didn't see this coming, man! We were gone until 9:00 last night and we had a permit for our visit. When we got home, I just figured they went to bed early and they'd parked the car in the shop. I'm not an early riser, so only just a few hours ago I went outside and discovered that no one was in the barns or outside. Then I figured I better check out their house before I call someone out here for nothing." Jimmy's face appeared redder than normal.

Andrew glanced at Darrell, "I think he's telling the truth. I've worked with him for a while now and I believe him."

Darrell looked thoughtful and then nodded. "Andrew, you told me that someone knew enough to remove the tracking units on the vehicles and attach them to farm trucks and tractors. Who would know how to do that?"

"John's son, Greg, actually worked at one of our intelligence centers. I checked and he didn't show up for work today. There's also a small patch of disturbed soil right behind the barn. It appears that someone dug something up there and then tried to camouflage the disturbed earth." Andrew shrugged and held out his hands. "I have no idea what could have been buried there."

Darrell nodded, "They must have been planning this for some time." Turning toward Jimmy again, "Do you have any idea what might have been buried there? Had there been any indication that they were planning on leaving?"

"I had no idea anything was buried anywhere. And like I said before, I didn't see this coming. Just before I left, John acted like he would see me after the weekend."

Andrew chimed in, "John seemed like a model citizen. He didn't like some of the changes, but he never gave me trouble about anything he had to do. I wouldn't have guessed that he would do something like this."

Jimmy looked at both men, "Do you think you'll be able to get him back here before harvest time? That is if we have a harvest."

Darrell shook his head, "Oh, he won't be coming back here! We have places set up for deserters where they won't be able to leave so easily. We'll assign someone else to this farm. You can stay here if you'd like Jimmy, but none of Mr. Bower's family will be coming back here."

He stood up, "I think we're about done here. I'll issue a notice to the entire state and all of the surrounding states. We'll catch them and make an example out of them so that others don't try to desert. Andrew, I'd appreciate you trying to find someone to take over this farm as soon as can be arranged."

Within ten minutes, Jimmy and Andromeda were the only ones left on the farm. Jimmy appeared pale. He shook his head, "I can't believe the family just took off and left us! I began to think John was the real thing! I thought that maybe there was something to this Christian stuff, but look at what a fake he turned out to be!"

Andromeda looked at him slowly and then said quietly, "Jimmy, look at it from his point of view. The government took everything from him that he had worked so hard all of his life to earn. He had no hope that his grandkids would have any chance to have what he had. If he cared about his family at all, he had to take off and try to protect them. He never told you he would be here when we got back."

Jimmy looked thoughtful for a minute. "Maybe you're right. I'm going to miss them though. If they can't come back here, I hope they do get away!"

"Me too. I wonder what they're doing now."

Chapter 23

John woke to the smell of pine needles. He looked around and got up slowly. He limped a little as he took a few steps. Then he walked normally to a log about fifty feet away from his sleeping family and sat down.

The air felt refreshingly cool. Light filtered through the trees from the east.

He looked up and quietly spoke toward the sky. "Am I doing the right thing? Do you really want me to put my family through this, Lord?"

He shook his head. "I'll never be able to go back to the home I grew up in. Things will never be the same again."

He put his head in his hands for a minute. Then he heard a familiar voice behind him. "Hey, there mister, what's a nice guy like you doing in a place like this?"

He turned to Anna and smiled. "Right now, I don't really know."

"Well if it helps you to feel better, I trust you and I think you're doing a great job!" She put her arms around him.

"Thanks, Honey, that helps."

The others were waking up. Tommy sat up and rubbed his eyes.

John felt no rush to leave. He and Jeff agreed to see how big of a wooded area they were in. They walked about a half a mile until they came to another field. Jeff looked across the field. "I think this area is big enough to camp in, but I don't think we should leave it till it's dark."

When they got back to camp, Greg had his slingshot out and sighted in on a squirrel. He let go and a moment later the squirrel fell out of the tree. John whistled, "It looks like you haven't forgotten how to use that thing!"

The day was clear, so they had some discussion about how to prepare the squirrel. They finally decided to clean and save it until they could cook it. About half of the adults went to forage for any food they could eat raw. They found a few nuts and some blackberries. They discovered a wet area where they found some cattail shoots they could eat.

After resting much of the day, they packed up and headed out by late afternoon. John's stomach felt a little empty but he knew they couldn't eat all of the food they had packed.

For the next two days, they continued this schedule of walking through as many meadows and fields as they could at night; during the day they would cover as much ground as they could in the forest. On the second day, clouds rolled in, so they started a fire and cooked a couple of squirrels that Greg had shot along with a goose that he killed.

Three days later, they were leaving a small woods at dawn. Across a small patch of grass, they saw a highway. After looking at it for a bit and realizing that the wooded area they were in seemed too small to spend the night safely, they decided that they would cross in small groups to the next line of trees.

John, Anna, and Tommy went first. They got to the next grove of trees, which stood about 100 yards away without incidence. Jeff, Sarah, and their kids went next. They took a little longer to cross. As they neared the highway, John spotted headlights coming around a curve a quarter of a mile away.

Jeff had not yet seen the car approaching, so he continued onto the highway. He got nearly halfway across when he saw the headlights approaching. He looked back briefly then continued walking normally.

He and the rest continued to the edge of the highway at a normal pace. The car slowed as it approached them and now it appeared obvious that it was a Federal police car. Jeff continued walking until the car stopped with its lights flashing and an officer got out.

He had his hand on his gun as he yelled, "Halt! I need to see your papers!"

Jeff turned and looked surprised. "We're just taking an early morning walk before we start working for the day. It's the best time for us to spend some time together."

"I still need to see your papers, sir!" the officer appeared to relax a bit. "There have been reports of illegal camping south of here, so we have to check everyone."

Jeff went toward him and reached for his wallet. As he approached, the officer held out his free hand to take the wallet. Just then, there came a slight whistling sound and a small thud. The officer stood for a second and then simply collapsed to the ground. Sarah instinctively gathered her children in her arms and covered their eyes.

Jeff could see the glint of a marble embedded almost halfway into his temple. Jeff quickly looked down the road to see if any other cars were in the area. Then he reached down and checked for a pulse. He stared at Sarah. His whole body felt numb. He couldn't believe how quickly things had escalated.

Sarah turned white in the face, "Is he...?" He nodded his head.

John came out from where he hid, "Jeff! Are you guys OK?!" Jeff just stared at him. "Jeff, we gotta move!" Jeff reached down and took the gun from the officer's hand and his flashlight from his belt.

John went to the car and turned off the lights and pulled the car well off the road. Everyone came out to the road. The women's eyes welled up as they tried to control their emotions and shield the children from the situation.

Tommy helped John to get the officer's body back into the car and propped him up to make him look like he just sat behind the wheel of his car.

John took a deep breath, "We've got to keep going fast and put some distance between us now! We'd better hit it hard most of the day."

Greg shook his head, "I'm sorry. I didn't know what else to do. I couldn't let him see Jeff's papers and radio for help."

"You did the right thing to protect them. There was nothing else to do."

As they traveled through the woods on the north side of the road, they came to a small river barely a half a mile in. John felt relieved that it was low due to the lack of rain they had throughout the area. He turned toward the group. "We're going to get wet for a while! We better carry the small kids."

He picked up Johnny and put him on his shoulders. Jeff picked up Samantha and Greg carried little Jenny.

John walked slowly downriver looking for any deep holes. The water flowed clear so they could see where the large rocks were. It made for slow going, but they went over a half a mile before John saw a creek feeding into the river.

He plodded up the creek for nearly another half a mile before he climbed up the bank and started through the forest. The towering trees were larger here so less underbrush got in their way.

John expressed relief about midday to realize that they were in a heavily forested area. By early afternoon, they had some cloud cover and they came upon a small lake. There was a flock of geese on the lake and Greg shot two of them.

John found some crickets and caught a few fish. After traveling for a couple of miles past the lake, they stopped and started a fire to cook their supper before dark. He remarked. "I'd just about forgotten what it feels like not to be hungry."

Greg looked at him, "Yeah, that's the most food we've had in a while."

Jeff rubbed his belly, "Sure feels different. Hey, John, think we should take turns keeping watch tonight?"

"Good idea, Jeff. I'll take the first shift."

Daylight streamed through the forest before any of them woke up naturally. They snacked on some of the food they had brought along for breakfast and then started walking again.

For the next few days, they hiked through heavily forested areas and found some small lakes where they were able to catch fish and shoot more geese.

After eating some goose and berries, Abby turned to Greg, "You know Honey, with these geese you get and berries, I actually feel human again."

"Yeah, I agree. I'm over the sore muscles and I kind of like sleeping out in the fresh air."

John looked at them, "We can't get too complacent, we're not out of the woods yet."

Tommy chuckled, "Good pun, Dad!"

John smiled, "Thanks son, but it's usually when people think they're doing good that they get blindsided with disaster."

"You're right, we don't know who else might be right behind us."

Jeff nodded, "Things have been going good for us so far, but we don't know what's in store for us tomorrow!"

Chapter 24

Two days later they were roasting two geese that Greg had shot. The clouds were thin and the breeze whispered lightly. The temperature remained a pleasant seventy-four degrees. They were sitting on logs talking and laughing together.

Suddenly Sarah said, "Shhh everybody! I heard something!"

As they quieted the kids and everyone held their breath, they all heard the unmistakable sound of a twig snapping. Then they could hear the sounds of footsteps.

They ran into the woods away from the sound. They had barely gotten the kids behind trees and shrubs when they saw movement on the other side of their camp.

They saw a young man and woman and two small children emerge from the woods. The man's clothes looked to be one size too big and he appeared to have not seen a barber in months. The woman had long auburn hair, but she lacked eye-catching features. The little boy's bright blond hair reflected the setting sun, while his older sister was a smaller version of their mom. They went over to the fire and when they saw the geese cooking, their faces brightened.

Seeing no one else following them, John and Tommy stepped out of hiding and went toward the ragged family. John cleared his throat, "Good afternoon!" At this, the man jumped and turned around.

"We're not going to hurt you," John reassured him. "You're welcome to stay and share our supper with us. We have plenty to go around."

The man looked back at the fire. "You have two geese just for the two of you?"

"No, there're more of us, but we heard you coming and hid. My name's John," John extended his hand.

"My name's Brian and this is my wife Rebecca. These are our kids, Zach and Hattie." Brian took John's hand. "We're mighty grateful for the offer of food. It's been weeks since we had a decent meal."

John called the others out of hiding. As they ate supper, Brian and his family repeatedly asked for more.

After supper, Rebecca shared their story. "We realized that we couldn't allow our kids to grow up under this system. We started out from southern Illinois about three and a half weeks ago. It's been slow going, but we walked as much as we could. Several days ago, some dogs were barking like they were trying to trail someone. We thought they were after us, but they went past us. We came to a river and it sounded like the dogs lost the trail at the river."

Greg glanced at John, then turned back toward Rebecca.

Rebecca continued, "We crossed the river further downstream, but we haven't found much to eat since we haven't found any fields to pick food in. We really appreciate your help and letting us eat with you."

Brian nodded, "Yeah, I appreciate this. I assume you're trying to make it to Canada like we are?"

"Yes, we're hoping to get there before it gets too cold. I hate to travel in too large of a group though. I think that would increase our exposure."

"Oh, I wouldn't expect to be able to travel with you. I agree with you that it would be safer to travel separately."

The kids played for the evening and the adults talked until they decided to go to bed.

In the morning, they shared a breakfast of nuts and a few berries. Then the two groups took slightly different directions as they both headed north.

Two days later, they were walking late in the afternoon. They hadn't found any lakes that day, so it began to look like supper might be slim. Suddenly, John stopped and they saw that the forest ended about a twenty yards ahead.

John looked out in the clearing and saw that they were on the edge of a field. Growing in the field were all kinds of truck crops. They could see melons and tomatoes, as well as beans and sweet corn. They could tell there were other crops further out in the field.

It looked so good! They were right in front of them. There were a few buildings about a quarter of a mile away. No sign of people could be seen anywhere.

Greg came over to him. "What do you think, Dad? I don't see anyone and some of those veggies would *really* hit the spot!"

"I don't know. Something about it just doesn't feel right."

They looked at it for a few more minutes, when they detected movement to their left. There were people coming out of the woods. They headed right into the field and looked like they were gathering as much as they could.

"Hey Dad, I think that's Brian and Rebecca and their kids! They seem to be doing all right."

He'd no sooner said that when about fifty yards past Brian, four men with assault rifles burst out of the woods. "Halt!" they yelled as they aimed at Brian and Rebecca.

Brian raised his hands and the rest of the family followed suit.

"Get on the ground!" one of the men ordered.

Once they were on the ground, the men handcuffed Brian and Rebecca and took them as well as their kids toward the house across the field.

John and Greg didn't say anything. As John turned, he realized the rest of his family was right behind him and had seen everything as well.

Anna shook her head, "It doesn't look like we'll have vegetables for supper."

John sighed, "I'm afraid you're right, Honey."

John led the way for another mile or two through the forest until close to dark before they camped for the night.

Tommy got his bed ready, "No fire tonight guys."

As they were preparing for sleeping Greg came over to John. "Hey Dad, I have trouble sleeping sometimes. I can't get the picture of that police officer out of my mind. I never thought I would ever have to do something like that."

"I understand Greg. Try to think of it as you saved Sarah and Jeff and their kids. You only did what you had to do,"

"Yeah, I suppose you're right."

John looked at the sky, "I just hope and pray that we all make it out okay. Otherwise, I may never be able to forgive myself for bringing everyone into this."

Greg nodded, "I hate to think about what they'll do to Brian and Rebecca."

Chapter 25

Ken Johnson sat at his desk looking over reports. He felt glad the air-conditioning worked well in his office. It had been one of the hottest Augusts he could remember.

It seemed to him that the atmosphere at his office had been tense the last couple of months. He shook his head as he read the latest crop report.

The drought had ruined the crops in his area. According to the report, the harvest would be less than half of what it had been last year.

In another report, the people trying to leave or rebel against the government had increased by nearly 200% in the last two months.

Amanda paged him, "Ken, Alex is on the line for you. He said he tried to call your cell last night, but he wasn't able to get through."

Ken picked up the phone. "Hello Alex. What can I do for you?"

"Ken, I know you can't control the weather, but I want you to know that some of those in charge are getting concerned. It appears that the control you have over the population is slipping. I know you're having some unrest and more and more people are disappearing."

"Look, I'm keeping most of the unrest to a minimum. It's just that people are concerned about the shortages! We have food shortages and gas shortages. Do you have any suggestions on how to keep people in line when they aren't getting enough food for their families?"

Alex paused for a few seconds, "I would suggest that you make an example out of the ones you catch and make sure everyone knows the consequences of their actions. You can't let the most productive members of society disappear and still expect to have enough goods and services."

"Hey, just remember that I had the best changeover in the country. You know me, Alex; I'm not going to just give up. I'll come up with a solution."

"I believe you, Ken, I know you will succeed."

After hanging up the phone, Ken sat and stared at the wall. He understood the food shortage, but the gas shortage seemed harder to figure out. He knew they were pumping more oil out of the Bakken oil fields than they had ever pumped. There should be plenty of gas and oil available.

Could someone be taking some for themselves?

According to what he had been told, everyone should be sharing in the wealth. They could use that extra oil to trade for food.

He shook his head. "That's not your business right now, Ken," he muttered.

He paged Amanda again. "Amanda, could you please get me the West Coast Director on the phone?"

A minute later he got connected, "Carl? This is Ken. I understand you had good crops this year."

"That's right. We had much better weather than yours."

"I would like to arrange a trade of produce for manufactured products. Do you think we could negotiate a deal?"

"Sure, Ken, send over your proposal."

"Thanks, Carl."

Five minutes after hanging up the phone, Amanda paged him again, "Ken, the North Central Federal Chief of Police is on the line."

"Good, I want to talk to him."

He hit the speaker button, "Hello, Aaron, I wanted to talk to you. I'm curious, have you made any headway into the killing of the officer in southern Wisconsin? That's an odd situation, I believe. He was killed by a marble, correct?"

"Yes, we didn't find him until several hours after he died. We got dogs on the trail right away. They seemed to find a trail that looked good until we got to a river. We went up and down the other side, but it's like whoever did it just went into the river and disappeared."

Ken cleared his throat, "I want the person responsible found!"

"We just don't have enough manpower to hunt down everyone that tries to get out."

"There was a farmer that deserted with his family. I believe his name is John Bower. Do you think he had anything to do with this?"

Aaron paused for a moment, "I don't know... We haven't found any sign of him or his family."

Ken frowned, "I was afraid he might be trouble. Do what you can to find him!"

"Hey, I do have some good news for you though."

"Well, I could use some of that today. What do you have?"

"About 50 miles north of where the officer had been killed, we caught a man and his family. They were trying to steal some produce from one of the best producing farms in Wisconsin."

"Could he be the killer?"

"We questioned him and he knows a bit about the dogs and stuff so he had been in the area. I don't think he did it though. He also said something about a larger group that had been heading toward Canada."

Ken pursed his lips, "Hmm, you can put him in the same area as where the officer was killed, you say?"

"I think so."

"If that's the case, can we pin the murder on him and make an example of him to make sure others don't try the same thing?"

"Maybe, but I don't think he did it."

Ken sat up in his chair, "Look, from now on, every case of rebellion needs to look like we solved it and appropriate punishment has been handed out. If people realize that they can't get away with any type of rebellion or desertion, we can start to curb it."

After a pause on the other end of the line, "If you say so, sir. But if I may speak frankly, I don't like it."

"Sometimes we have to do things we don't like."

"You might be right, though. It could keep any rebellion under wraps."

After Ken finished his conversation with Aaron, he sat at his desk and thought about how things were going. He lived in a mansion and had servants to cook for him and to clean up after him. He had a position of power and he could go anywhere he wanted to.

So, why did he feel like something was wrong? Maybe things weren't as good for everyone as he thought they would be when the government took control and made sure things were equal for everyone.

Why were so many people risking their lives to try to leave? Maybe it would just take more time.

He decided he needed a break. He might want to go see the Wisconsin Dells this weekend.

He would see if Amanda would go with him. They always seemed to have a good time together.

Ken shook his head, "Back to the situation at hand. Where could John Bower and his family have gone? That many people can't just disappear!"

Chapter 26

The next morning John got up early. Light just began to penetrate the dense forest. The morning air felt cool but comfortable. He surveyed his sleeping family around him. Then the previous day's events came into his consciousness.

He reached over and gently touched Anna. "Hey, Anna! We better get up and get going!"

"What's the rush? It feels awful early."

"I know, but after yesterday, I think we better get away from here."

Anna sat up and yawned, "Yeah, you're probably right."

John woke up the others as quietly as he could.

Tommy stood up. "Dad, do ya think they found out about us from Brian and Rebecca?"

"I dunno, but we have to assume they did."

"Boy, that's a real shame the way they got caught."

"Yeah, I hated to see that."

Anna got out the rest of the bread and nuts they had and divided them among the group. They ate in silence.

Once everyone got their packs, they took off and headed northwest. For the next several days, they continued a brisk pace, stopping where they thought they could to get food.

They used the fishing pole and the slingshot often. After several days at this pace, much of the time they were in forested areas and there were fewer fields.

They crossed roads occasionally. They did this in small groups like before. Only now, they crossed them without incidence. The roads were often miles apart.

After a couple of days, John led at a slower pace. When they came to a creek or shallow river, they seldom crossed directly, but walked in them for a ways, just in case they were being tracked.

The end of summer approached. They took it a little slower and spent more time trying to find food. When they found food, and if clouds were present, they would start a fire and cook a meal.

They had one day that it rained. When it started to rain, some of the adults held out their arms and looked up to let the rain run down their face. "It's been a long time since I've felt rain!" Sarah exclaimed.

Jeff smiled, "I know what you mean. It feels good!"

Everyone in the group had lost weight. The smaller kids still got carried from time to time, but they marched on without complaining.

It had been two weeks after Brian and Rebecca were captured. The family was walking in the middle of the afternoon. John turned to Anna, "I sure hope we don't have much further to go."

"Yeah, me too."

John walked beside her for a few more seconds, "We need to reach Canada before it gets too cold."

"I know, we don't have any winter clothes with us."

John nodded, "My thoughts exactly."

Anna looked back at Johnny, "I'm really concerned about the little kids."

Tommy came up behind them, "At least it's not as hot as it has been. Actually, these last few days have been quite comfortable."

Anna smiled, "I'm thankful for that!"

John stepped over a small tree trunk, "I haven't seen any sign of civilization today. What say we stop a little early and have a fire this evening?"

Tommy nodded, "That sounds good."

They were in an older forest, so the underbrush thinned out. It didn't take long to find some rocks to form a circle with and start a fire. Greg shot a few squirrels that they were able to cook.

They had finished eating supper and were relaxing around the fire as it died out.

Tommy finished chewing his last bite, "You know, Dad, this has actually been kind of fun these last few days."

Sarah nodded, "I know what you mean, Tommy. I wish we could do something like this more often. But not under these circumstances of course!"

"Hey, I've got an idea," said Greg, "When we get set up where we're going, why don't we do a camping trip every year in memory of this?"

Anna looked at John, "That might be a good idea. I think we've all grown a lot closer through this."

Abby winced, "I don't know. I think I want a nice mattress to sleep on if we do anything like this again."

John grinned, "What I miss the most... is toilet paper!"

Everybody chuckled.

Jeff had been silent for a while, but now he spoke up. "You know, our lives will never be the same. I'm afraid my kids will never see my parents again. We'll have to learn a whole new culture…possibly even a new language! If we make it out of here, we won't be going back to the same lives we left."

"You're right," John responded. "I can't even imagine the loss you must be feeling with your parents. However, I'm so grateful that we all have each other and that's the most important thing."

Everyone sat silent with their own thoughts for a moment, then John spoke again, "I s'ppose we should go to bed. We ought to get an early start in the morning."

The next morning, a thick fog had rolled in and they had trouble seeing more than 30 feet in front of them. Greg got up early and shot several squirrels. With the fog, they decided to start a fire and cook the squirrels for a small breakfast.

After breakfast, the fog obscured their vision but they took off anyway. John checked the compass frequently to make sure they were still on track. The fog persisted until close to noon when they came to a highway. John looked both ways, then he spotted a car heading their way. John backed into the edge of the wood until it passed.

After it went by, Tommy touched John's arm, "Dad, did you see that?!"

"What do you mean?"

"That car had a Canadian license plate!"

John's eyes widened, "Are you sure?"

"I'm sure, I think we made it!"

John looked up and down the highway, "Let's not get too excited yet. We don't want to risk everything too soon."

Tommy looked at John, "What do you suggest?"

"Let's walk a bit farther and make sure we're in Canada before we come out."

Tommy grinned, "So you're saying we're not out of the woods yet?"

"Very funny!"

They walked a few more miles that day and crossed two roads. Each time they waited by the roadside to see if a car would come by. At the first road, they waited nearly a half an hour and no cars came by.

At the second road, a car came by about ten minutes after they got there. They were all eager to look at the rear of the car as it passed. There could be no mistaking that it had a Canadian license plate.

After discussing the situation, they decided to stay hidden for another day while they headed farther north, just to make sure they wouldn't lose everything they had gone so far to accomplish.

They camped that night well in the woods but started a fire to cook some fish they had managed to catch.

The next morning, they got up and headed out early. When they came near a thicket of thorn bushes, John walked back to Jeff. "Hey, Jeff, you probably better ditch that gun and flashlight that you got from that officer. It might not be good to be caught with that stuff on you."

"Yeah, you're right." Jeff pulled the magazine out of the gun and tossed it into the bushes. About 200 yards away he tossed the gun and flashlight into the bushes.

They walked for a couple of miles until they came to another road. They walked parallel to the road while keeping mostly hidden in the woods. They made slow progress because of all of the underbrush, but by early afternoon they could see a gas station coming up.

As they neared the back of the gas station, they saw a curve in the road. Once they could see past the curve, it became obvious that a small town was just ahead of them.

John looked back at the others, "Well guys, I guess this is the moment of truth."

Jeff stared at him for a minute, "Boy, it'd be a real bummer if we did this all in vain."

"I agree, but we'll find out soon."

John insisted that everyone else remain hidden while he and Tommy walk into town and see what they could find. He and Tommy cleaned up and brushed their hair as well as they could, then they walked to the edge of the road.

Chapter 27

The day was clear, and though the sun shone brightly, the temperature reached only the low 70's. Most of the area around the town looked wooded and it appeared that the town survived a lot on tourism.

John jumped the first time a car passed them. "Tommy, it sure seems strange to walk along the road and not try to hide every time a car goes by."

"Yeah, I know what you mean, Dad."

They got into town without anyone questioning them. The town was a quaint town with old brick buildings near downtown. It had been well-kept and most of the buildings were filled with small businesses.

They passed a bait and tackle store, several clothing stores and, as they turned a corner, they spotted a small pawnshop on a side street. They decided that would be their best bet.

They entered the shop and saw only one other customer in the store. He appeared to be an outdoorsy type who looked at a small assortment of fishing gear. John and Tommy pretended to look at a couple of chainsaws until the other man left without making a purchase.

Then they approached the counter. The man at the counter was an older man with a mostly bald head and a medium build except for a bit of a belly that hung over his belt. He had a kind face, but his expression showed he meant business.

John went up to the counter and asked, "Do you buy silver?"

"Sure! What do you have?"

John pulled out some of the silver coins he had and laid them on the counter. The man pulled out a magnifying glass and examined them. "I'll be glad to buy these, but I'll need to see your ID."

John hesitated for a moment, then he pulled out his passport and laid it on the counter.

The man picked up the passport and looked at it. He then looked John and Tommy up and down and noticed their lean appearance, their beards, and their worn and soiled clothes.

He got up and went to the door, locked it, and turned his sign around. When he came back to the counter, he finally spoke again, "You're going to need other IDs in the future. I know a guy who can get you the proper Canadian identification, but it's not cheap. You've been through a lot already - I'm not going to try to take advantage of you. I feel sorry for you and for what happened to your country."

John stood there for a moment. He stared into the man's kind eyes. He glanced at Tommy with tears welling in his eyes, swallowed hard, and then spoke. "Thank you. I know we'll need some other papers. We need papers for other people too."

"How many others are we talking?"

"Altogether, there are seven adults and five kids."

The man whistled. "You walked all of the way out with that many and five kids too?! That's amazing! Occasionally we get some young people that got out, but I've never seen such a large family make it so far. I hate to tell you this, but it's going to take a bit more than you have here to get identification papers and passports for that many."

John nodded, "I figured that."

"It's not just a matter of printing the forms anymore. Someone with incredibly good skills has to enter you into the system, and that's what costs so much."

John pursed his lips, "I have more available. Can we cash in a little silver now so we can get some groceries and necessities, and then come back tomorrow to discuss the details?"

"Tomorrow's Sunday, and I'm closed on Sunday. It'll be Monday morning before I'll be in again. I'll give you cash for what you have here. There's a hotel at the end of Main Street. You can stay there for a couple of nights and recuperate. I know the owner. I'll call him and he'll give you a good rate and won't ask for any ID. When you talk to him, tell him that you're the ones that Larry talked to him about."

John chuckled, "I had no idea what day of the week it was. It would be great to shower and sleep in a real bed again!"

After pocketing the cash Larry gave him, he and Tommy went to the store a bought some cold meat and fruit. They carried the stuff back to where the others were. The food disappeared in a hurry.

After eating, they walked into town and went to a discount clothing store first. They each purchased a change of clothing and headed for the hotel. John went in and requested three rooms. He told the man at the counter, "Larry told us to come here to get some rooms for the night."

"Oh, yes, he called me and told me you would be coming." The man looked in his book. "I have three rooms ready for you on the second floor. Do you need any rollaway beds for the children?"

"If each of the rooms has two beds in them, we could use one rollaway bed."

"I'll have that sent up. Is there anything else you would like?"

John smiled, "Yes, could you tell us where a good restaurant is?"

After getting directions to the restaurant, John paid him for the rooms.

They each went to their rooms. The rooms were old and the furniture looked like it had been bought at second-hand stores, but they were clean and smelled good. They spent the next hour and a half taking turns in the shower and grooming. By the time they were done, they looked quite respectable.

When everyone got ready, they headed down the street toward the restaurant. As soon as they walked in the door, they were greeted by an aroma that they had not smelled for what seemed like a lifetime.

They got appetizers and ordered their meals. The food tasted delicious, but none of them could finish their meals. Greg leaned back in his chair, "Man, that tasted great, but I can't believe how quickly I got full!"

Abby nodded, "Honey, I think all of our stomachs have shrunk!"

Jeff sighed, "It sure feels good to have a full stomach again."

By now it was a dark and cool night, but quite comfortable. They went back to their rooms and John and Anna laid on their bed. John turned on the TV to catch up on the news.

He started to watch the news and the next thing he knew it was four o'clock in the morning and he woke up to the sound of sirens. He jumped up and took a couple of steps when he realized the sirens were on a movie that played on TV. He turned it off and looked over at Tommy's bed. Tommy remained sound asleep.

Anna woke up, "Is something wrong dear? I felt you jump out of bed."

"No, I heard sirens on TV, and in my sleep, I thought the police were after us. Actually, I think everything is better than it has been for a long time."

He crawled back into bed and took her in his arms. Before long, they both fell asleep again and the next thing he knew it was 7:30 in the morning and the sun shone in the window.

The hotel served a continental breakfast, so they all had an ample meal. Since they would have a whole day before they could meet with Larry, they decided to explore the town. They walked a few blocks and they came to a church that had people filing in. It was a small quaint wooden church with an old fashioned steeple.

After discussing it, they decided to go in. The people were warm and friendly. After the service, they got lunch and this time, used a little more self-control when ordering.

They spent the rest of the day exploring the town and relaxing in the park. John and Anna watched a movie in their room that evening while Tommy took all of the kids out for ice cream at a local ice cream parlor.

The next morning, they all went to the pawnshop. As soon as they entered, Larry looked up. A minute later his face lit up. "My, my, you've changed since you were in here the last time. It took me a second to recognize you. You certainly look a lot better."

He got up and locked the door again and then sat down. "I talked to my guy and he wants to remain anonymous so you'll deal through me."

John nodded, "That's fine. I feel like we can trust you."

"I'm glad you feel that way. I think you can keep the same names that you have now. We'll just have to build a background for all of you along with past addresses."

John took more silver up to Larry. It took close to half of the silver they had with them to pay for the documents to be made. "How long will it take to receive them?"

"They'll probably take about a week. You'll need to hang around here till then."

During the next week, they got a couple of changes of clothes for all of them as well as other necessities. Just as Larry had said, the passports and other identification papers came in that week. At Larry's suggestion, they destroyed their old ones and memorized the information about themselves that had been entered into the system.

As they left the pawnshop, Anna looked at John, "Honey, you think these new passports will work?"

"I hope so. We'll soon find out."

Chapter 28

It was early September. Nights were cool and the days were beautiful. They had become well acquainted with the little town.

John found a place that had an international telephone. He pulled out the worn slip of paper that he had carried with him for over a month. He dialed the number and heard the phone ring on the other end.

After a couple of rings, he heard a voice he hadn't heard for quite some time, "Hola!"

"Jim? It's John Bower!"

"John! How are you doing? Are they letting you call me? Where are you calling from?"

John proceeded to briefly tell Jim the story of where they were and how they got out. Then he went on, "Jim, you said to contact you if I ever needed something. I have my whole family with me and I don't have the farm anymore. Is there any chance you could use a little help until we could get settled again?"

"John, I've got plenty of ground. If you can get plane tickets, you won't have to worry about any other expenses. I'd love to have you and your family help me until you can get back on your feet."

After discussing the details, John hung up. He went back to Larry and cashed in most of the rest of his gold and silver. Then he asked Larry if he could pay him to help make plane reservations. They used Larry's credit card and John paid him back for the cost of them. It took the majority of what John had left.

The next day John and his entire family caught a bus to the airport. John felt apprehensive as he presented his new identification. However, they got through security with no problems. They flew out on September the 10th.

John settled into the seat as the plane took off. Once they were in the air, his thoughts went back to the last few years. "I've lost almost everything that I worked so hard to get all of my life. It's hard to believe the tough times I've had to go through."

Anna leaned her head against his shoulder as she closed her eyes. John looked down at her. Then he looked around and could see all three of his children. He noticed his grandchildren talking and laughing with each other. "No," he thought, "I haven't lost everything, I've saved everything."

Chapter 29

Abdul had a visitor on September the 8th. He brought an envelope. Abdul opened the letter and it had just one sentence on it. The message read, "Bake the cake at 10:00 on September the 11th."

He knew what it meant. He stood and stared at the note for a minute. Then he went out for a while. When he came back to the house, he told Ashley that he wanted to talk to her. "Ashley, I have a permit for you to take the boys and go see your parents in Kansas. I want you to leave tomorrow and go stay with them for a week or so."

"Abdul! I don't get it. I haven't seen them for years! Why do you want me to go see them now? And what about you, don't you want to come?"

Shaking his head, he said, "I'm not going to answer any of your questions. You just have to do as I say without asking any questions. Do you understand?"

She had only seen him this stern when she told him she had become a Christian. She stared at him for a full minute. Abdul's expression did not change. Finally, Ashley spoke, "Ok, I'll do as you say, but I don't feel good about this."

Ashley thought about what Abdul said. She would like to see her parents again; she hadn't left on good terms with them before. She did want them to know that she had changed. She also wanted them to be able to see their grandkids.

The next day, she left as ordered and it seemed that Abdul hugged the boys a little longer than usual.

After they left, Abdul became especially devout in his prayers. On the morning of September 11th, he went down to the basement. He pulled the cover off of the apparatus he had been working on. He knew that in other major cities other men were doing the same thing.

He thought of his sons. He also thought of the paradise waiting for him. He believed that what he was about to do would earn him great rewards in paradise.

He pulled out a key that he always kept with him. He did some final preparations and then inserted the key. He kept an eye on his watch and observed the last few minutes tick by.

At precisely 10:00, he turned the key. The flash of light hardly registered on his brain.

Chapter 30

Ken traveled to southern Illinois to meet with some of his area directors on the morning of September 11th. He had driven about 50 miles from the city when he saw an odd site in his rearview mirror. A large cloud of smoke appeared above the city and morphed into the shape of a giant mushroom.

It took only a moment for it to register with him what had happened. He immediately tried to call his office but could not get through. He tried to call Alex in Washington and discovered that his cell phone had no signal.

He drove about 10 miles farther and found a gas station. He pulled in and went inside. When he entered, he noticed that the inside appeared darker than he expected. A man stood behind the counter and he went up to him.

"Do you have a landline that works?"

"No, I tried to call someone about 15 minutes ago when the electricity went out, but the phone was dead too. What's going on here?! Somebody in the government better do something about it soon or nobody's going to be able to get gas from here."

Ken didn't tell him his name. He wasn't sure what to do now. He certainly didn't want to head to Chicago and risk getting radiation poisoning. He decided to keep heading south and see if he could find some way to contact someone in Washington.

After driving south for about an hour, he came to a small town. He pulled in to a gas station that had its lights on. Ken went inside and saw a young man working behind the counter.

"I see the electricity is on here, do you have a phone that works?"

"No," the man at the counter said. "We only have electricity because there had been a generator left here and we got it started. If you need gas, the local police chief said I could only allow people to take three gallons per person."

"Why is that?"

"We don't know when we'll get more gas. There have been some reports that Chicago got hit with a nuclear bomb, but I wonder if the government did it just to create a crisis."

Ken looked him in the eyes, "I can assure you that the government had nothing to do with this, but I'll take whatever gas I can get. Here's my card to verify that I'm allowed to be traveling and can get gas."

The man looked at it and looked at Ken. "I'm so sorry sir. I didn't realize who you were. I suppose you can get all the gas you need. Do you know what's going on?"

"Not yet. I haven't been able to contact anyone."

He drove on for a while, not sure where to go. He wished there was some way to communicate with somebody and figure out what had happened. He started to get hungry now. He wondered if his card would work at any restaurants if any were open.

He entered a medium-sized town and went to the first stoplight. It wasn't working, but there stood a policeman directing the little traffic they had. He stopped and asked directions to the police station. It was only three blocks away, so he arrived there quickly.

When he went inside, he realized they either had electricity or they were using a generator. He went to the counter and asked to see the police chief. After being directed to his office, he went to the door and knocked.

The chief opened the door and recognized Ken immediately. "Hello, sir. I didn't expect to see you. We heard what happened in Chicago but we're not sure what's going on with the rest of the country."

"How do you have electricity? Do you use a generator or is there power here?"

"We have a generator sir. We also have a shortwave radio set up and we're trying to find out what happened across the country. By the way, you may not remember me. My name is Keith." The chief said as he held out his hand.

Ken took his hand. "It appears you're doing a great job at maintaining order here, considering the circumstances."

At that point, an officer entered the office. "Sir, we've been able to contact several shortwave radios throughout the country. There aren't a lot out there because it appears most of the country is without power. Most of the radio operators are using generators."

Keith looked at him "What do we know so far?"

"Well, it appears that nuclear devices were detonated in major cities throughout the United States. Washington also got hit with one. Much of the power grid throughout the country has been damaged. We don't know of anyone in DC that's still capable of delivering direction. There are reports that Air Force One left the country last night. Those reports have not been confirmed."

Keith turned towards Ken, "Well, sir, it appears that you're in charge for the time being. What do you suggest we do?"

This was unknown territory for Ken. There was no protocol for this. "Well, the first thing we need to do is accurately assess the situation. What resources do we have? Do we have any food resources?"

Over the next couple of days, the two men worked closely with one another as they worked to restore order. Keith helped Ken get a place to stay and made sure he got food.

Within a week, their reserves were getting dangerously low. No supply trucks were running and reports from around the country talked of anarchy reining in many areas. People did whatever it took to get food.

Even in town, Ken could sense the growing dissension. Some people came into the station and complained about thefts and break-ins. Then a couple of officers didn't show up for work. Within two weeks, the force slimmed down to half its former size. Complaints weren't coming in as fast, but evidence abounded of even more unrest. A couple of dead bodies were found just outside of town.

Two days later, Keith didn't show up for work. Ken and three other officers were the only ones that showed up that day. The three officers went out on patrol and never returned.

Ken sat alone in the office. Reviewing the way people had been looking at him, he decided it would be best to leave town and go somewhere where he might not be known. He had a half a tank of gas and got over 200 miles south of there before he ran out.

He walked to the nearest farmhouse and when no one came to the door, he went inside and noticed a foul smell from the living room. He cautiously looked through the doorway to the living room. On the floor lying in pools of blood were a man, a woman, and three children. Clothes and other belongings were strewn about the room.

He went outside and threw up next to the back porch.

As he walked away, he wondered how people could sink so low to do something like that. Didn't people have any sense of right and wrong?

After hiking along the road for two more miles, he came to a small town. As he passed the first house, he heard leaves crunch behind him and felt a sharp jab in his ribs.

"Give me your shoes!" The voice sounded young.

As he started to bend down, Ken whirled around and grabbed the gun. Instinctively he twisted it away from his side. There was an explosion and he felt the gun jerk.

He found himself face to face with a young boy in the late stages of puberty. For an instant, they stared into each other's eyes, then the boy's eyes glazed over as he fell backward.

Ken looked at the body at his feet and then glanced at the gun in his hand. He ducked behind the next house and looked down the road. After a few minutes, he realized no one was coming his way.

His growling stomach reminded him that he hadn't eaten since breakfast. He checked the clip on the 9mm.

"Six rounds left. That should be enough to get food with." He considered his options for a minute. "If things get much worse, I better make sure to save one round for myself."

I trust that you've enjoyed this novel. I hope that it entertained you as well as made you think. If so, I'd appreciate if you would post a review on Amazon.

By posting a review, you can help other readers to find my book.

I highly value your review!

Thank you,

Robert

www.ingramcontent.com/pod-product-compliance
Lightning Source LLC
Chambersburg PA
CBHW051527260626
47170CB00003B/825

* 9 7 8 0 5 7 8 7 3 3 5 2 4 *